Ethics in Competitive & Recreational Sport

Activity Workbook

Margery Holman
University of Windsor

Kendall Hunt
p u b l i s h i n g   c o m p a n y

Quotes on pages 17, 42, 51, 55, 57, and 65 from *The Windsor Star*, August 2009, May 31, 2011, October 27, 2007, and November 21, 2009. Copyright by *The Windsor Star*. Reprinted by permission.

Cover images © Shutterstock, Inc.

Kendall Hunt
publishing company

www.kendallhunt.com
Send all inquiries to:
4050 Westmark Drive
Dubuque, IA 52004-1840

Copyright © 2011 by Kendall Hunt Publishing Company

ISBN 978-0-7575-9460-1

Printed in the United States of America

10 9 8 7 6 5 4 3 2

Contents

Preface   **v**

Sample Course Outline   **vii**

Chapter 1 **Introduction**   **1**

Process for Ethical Decision Making 3

Four Factors That Impede Ethical

Decision Making 4

What Is Ethics? .5

 Ethical Terms. 5

Ethics and the Law 6

How to Apply Ethics to Sport 7

 Moral Values 9

Application of Ethical Terms 11

Summary .12

Chapter 2 **Fair Play Principles and Codes of Conduct** . . **17**

Code of Ethics .18

 What Is a Code of Ethics? 18

 Why a Code of Ethics? 18

 Who Is Responsible to the Code

 of Ethics? 18

Content 19

Chapter 3 **Youth Sport**   **21**

Athlete Drop Out: When Does Ethics Factor in? 23

Sample Case Analysis. 24

 Additional Cases 24

Introduction to Discrimination in Sport   **27**

Chapter 4 **Gender in Sport**   **29**

Facts to Help in Decision Making 31

Summary .32

Chapter 5 **Race and Ethnicity**   **33**

Chapter 6 **Disability**   **37**

Chapter 7   **Commercialization**   **41**

Colleges/Universities 42

Opponents 46

Officials. 47

Fans. 49

Chapter 8   **Performance Enhancing Substances and Practices**   **51**

How Do Ethics Guide Our Actions? 51

Policy 56

Chapter 9   **Violence in Sport**   **57**

The "Everyone Else Does It" Argument 58

The "Good" Foul/Penalty 59

Violence and Contact Sport 60

Hazing 62

Chapter 10   **Gambling and Sport**   **65**

Animals for Entertainment: With and Without Gambling 66

Chapter 11   **Organizational Ethics**   **67**

Responsible Recruitment, Management, and Retention of Personnel: Being a Good Employer/Being a Good Employee 67

Creating an Ethical Organization 69

Maintaining the Values of Your Organization 70

Additional Note: Research Ethics 71

Appendices   **73**

Appendix A 73

Appendix B 79

Appendix C 83

Appendix D 171

Website Resources 171

Case Analysis Forms 172

Preface

This workbook has been designed to serve as a teaching tool in an introductory ethics course for college and university students in a sport, recreation, or physical activity program. It is constructed on the basis of a 12-week semester with 3 lecture hours per week (36 hours).

Disclaimer: All cases cited in this workbook are fictional. While some cases may have been motivated by situations that are common in sport and physical activity, no actual set of circumstances are represented in the cases as presented.

CHAPTER (1)

Introduction

The purpose of this chapter is to provide some introductory material and course resources to help with the organization of the class.

Ethics curriculum has grown in recent years across multiple disciplines. For example, we see ethics courses in business, engineering, education, medical schools, law, and kinesiology. Of course, the pinnacle from which we all borrow materials to tailor courses specific to our discipline is philosophy. But a persistent question that eludes a universal response is "can ethics be taught?"

The underlying principle for this course will be that moral behavior is learned and therefore, it can be taught. This can be accomplished by following a number of guidelines. As a student, you will need to:

- Learn to ask questions and decide which voice of authority (or combination of authorities) you wish to believe. There will always be a variety of opinions about situations that demand an ethical response. You need to form your own opinion that reflects your values.

Example: Fighting in hockey is good.

(?) EXERCISE #2
Debate the example statement shown above after reading the information that follows.

Individuals who have played or watched hockey may not have given this statement much thought. Your response is likely to be a reflex based on what you have learned from your experiences, and most probably from the opinions of the people with whom you have interacted. But, there is a time when we need to question those opinions, if not to form a new one, to at least understand the reasons we hold a particular perspective. Ask yourself why you agree or disagree with this statement. Ask yourself why someone who adopts the opposite position might agree or disagree with this statement. What are the pros and cons about fighting in hockey? Does this statement apply to everyone who plays hockey,

(?) EXERCISE #1
Debate the question, "Can ethics be taught?"

1

regardless of age, sex, commercialization and other characteristics? What justifies your position? How does your response reflect your values?

- Avoid adopting another's position as your position without asking the questions that need to be asked. Often people assume the position of the first person who speaks or of the person they know or admire. There is no guarantee that the viewpoint of others will represent your opinion or your values.

- Search for strengths and weaknesses in the arguments of others, ensuring that you have all of the information before forming your own opinion and that the information you receive is relevant to the situation under debate.

- Become a critical thinker. Critical thinking requires that individuals engage in **cognitive dissonance**, an intellectual exercise that moves decisions from a superficial examination to an in-depth analysis of the facts and options available in response.

Example: Fighting in hockey is good. Maybe it is ... Maybe it is not...

Individuals in sport and physical activity are faced with situations on an almost-daily basis either personally, through observation, or from the media reports on the world of sport. As future or even current professionals in the field, none of us will ever be "put out of business" when it comes to responding to ethical questions. We see a variety of violent activity, doping infractions, personal bad behavior, eligibility violations, or athlete exploitation as examples of questionable ethical behavior. Coaches, administrators, officials, athletes, and spectators are more commonly the focus of unethical behavior, but there are many others, such as athletic therapists, sponsors, alumni, or educators. Unethical behavior occurs in school sport at all levels from elementary to university, club sport, and in semi-professional and professional sport organizations. These groups collectively often are referenced as the **stakeholders**. They and the mission of their organization (reason for their existence) must be taken into account when analyzing a case. Analysis of a case therefore requires the identification of all stakeholders. Whether they are affected by any decision directly or indirectly, consideration of their interests must be part of the analysis. The following provides a description of how the NCCP model works.

DEFINITION

COGNITIVE DISSONANCE is a problem-solving process. It is engaging in a personal debate with yourself (cognitive–using your mind) whereby you challenge (dissonance–disagreeing with yourself) your moral values, examine the issues of a conflict, and determine the course of action needed to reflect the values that are important to you.

DEFINITION

STAKEHOLDERS are those individuals who have an interest or investment in the organization and its affairs for the benefit of themselves, the organization, or mutual advancement.

Process for Ethical Decision Making

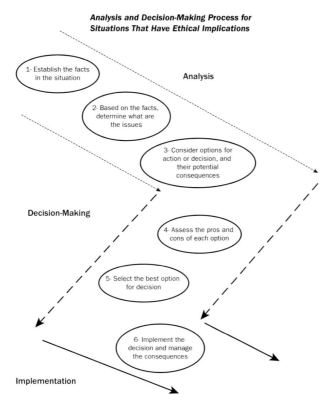

From *Making Ethical Decisions Course Facilitator Resources* by Coaching Association of Canada. Copyright by Coaching Association of Canada. Reprinted by permission.

The decision making process begins with an analysis of the case. The first step is to identify all of the facts. This requires a perspective from all parties involved, clarification of any ambiguities, and exposing any inconsistencies. Once the facts have been determined, the issues of dispute can be established.

Following the establishment of facts, a course of action may begin to unfold. This involves a shift from analysis to indentifying the decision options available, and the pros and cons of each guided by personal and organizational values. This is critical in establishing a justification for the decision that is eventually made. It is here that the value of having identified stakeholders emerges. With each option available, the way in which it will be implemented and the effect that it will have on each of the stakeholders must be considered to reach a fair decision for all. This may require a prioritization of stakeholder interests on a case by case basis, recognizing that decisions may be more relevant for one stakeholder over another, i.e., student-athlete education versus sponsor expectations where it would be more important to consider the educational success of a student athlete than the profit margins for a sponsor. To complete the decision making, the best option must be selected along with an understanding of the reasons for the selection and a justification for the choice. This stage requires that those who are responsible for the decision must be accountable for their judgment.

Once the best option has been identified, it is time to move to the implementation phase. The decision must be communicated to the appropriate individuals along with expectations for implementation. This stage also requires an evaluation of the process that ensures that the right decision has been made and consequences—anticipated or unanticipated—are managed in a positive way.

DEFINITION

ACCOUNTABILITY is taking responsibility for decisions and their outcome with an obligation to accept the consequences.

Accountability makes it important that you know why you make the decisions or the choices that you make. If you make a good decision, it is much easier to accept responsibility, because others will see the benefits of that decision or choice. But if you make a bad decision, it is much more difficult to accept responsibility. This is when athletes, coaches, and others "make excuses," or attempt to deflect the blame onto someone else. While the following example demonstrates how an athlete refuses to be accountable for actions taken during a competition, there are a number of additional issues that can be discussed in this case either now or later in the workbook.

> **Example:** A boxed lacrosse player shoves a player into the boards after a play has been made, causing an injury that requires the player to be carried off the playing surface. The injured player was unable to return to the game, but recovered to play in the team's next competition. The offending player was ejected from that game with a match penalty and given an additional three game suspension by the league's review board. When interviewed by the media, the penalized player complained that the officials were unfair in stating that there was no intent to injure and that the injury was exaggerated by the opponent to draw the penalty.

(?) EXERCISE #3
Accountability in lacrosse.

In small groups, discuss how the following stakeholder should be accountable in lacrosse example. Identify the accountability of the penalized player, (1) the coach of the penalized player, (2) the coach of the injured player, (3) officials, and the (4) review board. Add any other factors that arise during your discussions.

Four Factors That Impede Ethical Decision Making

Adaptation from "Strategy for Ethical Decision-Making". Copyright © 1994 Association for Healthcare Philanthropy Foundation.

Association for Healthcare Philanthropy Foundation (AHPF) has identified four factors that impede ethical decision making. These are self-indulgence, self-protection, self-deception, and self-righteousness.

1. **Self-indulgence** occurs when values are sacrificed by such temptations as money, power, sex, or the win. You must ask what price, if any, will be attached to your values. An example of this in sport would be an athlete

accepting an under the table payment from an alumnus to attend a particular university to play a sport.

2. **Self-protection** occurs when people behave in ways to protect themselves from undesirable consequences, based on their behaviors or decisions even if those consequences are just. An example of this in sport would be to cover up academic dishonesty.

3. **Self-deception** occurs when people find a way to justify a decision or action without seeing the negative implications or the ethical values that may have been violated. An example in sport would be using an overage player in a competition where the coach explains that without doing so the team would have to forfeit and that the athlete would only play if needed.

4. **Self-righteousness** occurs when individuals with a sense of superiority believe that their opinions are right without consideration of the viewpoint of others. An example in sport would be that athletic scholarships are either right or wrong without looking at the pros and cons associated with them.

What Is Ethics?

Ethics is a classification of philosophy. It is represented by a set of moral principles that provide a code by which behavior and decisions are guided. A moral code is comprised of values that represent what is good versus what is bad. For the purpose of this workbook, the terms ethical and moral will be interchangeable. The main theory that will be used is Theory for Respect for Persons along with the introduction of additional independent principles.

Ethical Terms

Principle of universalization states that equal respect is due to all human beings.

Self-defeating test questions whether an individual can consent to others acting simultaneously according to the same rule that you use without undermining your own ability to act in accordance with it—for example in sport, if you manipulate a rule to gain an advantage, can you consent to others manipulating the same rule to gain the same advantage without erasing the advantage that you had intended to achieve by manipulating this rule? If not, why would you engage in this type of behavior?

Means-end principle states that those actions are right that treat individuals as an end and not simply as a means to an end.

Moral agency offers a person freedom to engage in behavior by unforced choices AND allows people to set their own goals and have the opportunity to achieve them.

Principle of forfeiture means you will have to forfeit your rights to freedom and well-being if you treat others as a means to an end.

Principle of equality requires others to be treated equally unless reasons exist for them to be treated otherwise; when someone's equality must be violated, this too must be done equally unless reasons exist for them to be treated otherwise.

Paternalism occurs when another person determines what is for an individual's own good, often using coercion to motivate someone to do something or refrain from doing something.

- Weak paternalism can be justified when individuals are unable to make an informed decision, often based upon such characteristics as age, knowledge, or mental capacity.

- Strong paternalism is difficult to justify, as it is an imposition on individuals capable of making an independent decision thus interfering with their freedoms and often, as in the case of sport, creating dependency.

Principle of double effect suggests that it is morally permissible to act when the result has two effects (one good and the other bad), if the bad effect is unavoidable to achieve the good effect + if the bad effect is unintended + if a convincing reason exists for taking this action.

Moral absolutism determines that certain actions are good or bad regardless of their outcome. For example, intentionally injuring an opponent's goalie when you know that they do not have a talented backup goalie is bad according to moral absolutism, even if it will ensure a win.

Ethics and the Law

Much of our morality has become embedded in our legal system, as our laws often reflect the values of society. For example, as a society we value life and therefore have laws to penalize those who kill other people. Yet, at the same time, laws can be immoral. At one time, laws existed that allowed slavery; a law in the Ontario Human Rights Code Section 19(2)allowed discrimination based on sex in sport that was in effect until 1986. Likewise, a person can be lawful and not ethical, while a person can also be ethical but not lawful. The easier situation with which to deal is prohibitions against behaviors that are in some way enforceable (legal approach), as opposed to admonitions of how people should think (ethical approach). So why do individuals behave in an ethical way? Is it belief in their values, fear of punishment, or fear of being judged badly by those around them? What would happen if there were no rules or laws? What would happen if there were no rules in a basketball game and no one to officiate? At what point does self-indulgence (see earlier definition) influence a contest in opposition to the original purpose of the competition?

ETHICS: Individual and collective social morality	**LAW:** A public expression of social morality
• precedes law • does not need law to exist • guides social morality, good or bad • gives meaning to law • not enforceable • actions or thoughts	• a legal code • a system of do's and don'ts, right or wrong • protections from harm to person or property • fear of punishment • enforceable • actions only • law sanctions morality • can do without the law if a set of standards are established and all agree to follow them
In sport, ethics represents the spirit of fair play—the values that lead to rules and regulations that guide sport.	In sport, law is represented by the organizational constitution, by-laws, sport specific rules, and regulations.

How to Apply Ethics to Sport

Adaptation from *Sport Ethics: Applications for Fair Play* by Angela Lumpkin, Sharon Kay Stoll, and Jennifer M. Beller. Copyright © 1994 C.V. Mosby, Inc.

Moral reasoning skills are an imperative element in making ethical decisions. Individuals do not have an innate capacity to do this. It requires a systematic process of reflecting on personal values and determining those principles by which one wants to live and in this case, engage in ethical experiences. This is the application of cognitive dissonance, whereby that personal debate is ongoing with every experience that challenges personal values. This process allows individuals to be consistent in the ways in which they respond to ethical dilemmas while also being fair, objective, and unbiased. Administrators, coaches, and others who follow this process become predictable in the way that they respond to ethical challenges. And they become the catalyst for moral development in those with whom they interact.

Findings from the research of Lumpkin, Stoll & Beller (1994) suggests that we are not adequately fostering moral development of our young people. Their research shows that athletes are less morally reasoned and morally developed than their peer population of non-athletes, with males less morally reasoned than females, although the gap is closing. We often see the results of this with questionable behavior on the fields/courts/ice/pool and other sites of competition as well as away from these venues. Unfortunately, it is not only the athletes who engage in such behavior. Moral development is the responsibility of athletic leaders and includes:

- **Moral education:** Course curricula, workshops, policy, and daily interactions are examples that provide opportunities to educate individuals about ethics in sport and physical activity. Through these educational experiences, individuals learn to examine their own values and the behaviors that reflect those values, an objective of this course.

- **Moral role models:** One of the best lessons learned is through observing the behaviors of others, particularly when that individual is held in high esteem. Leaders can make the choice of whether or not they wish to model behavior that is based on sound moral principles. Those entrusted to their care will learn, and in all probability, adopt the values observed in their experiences.

- **Moral environment:** A moral environment is one in which individuals are exposed to situations that offer an opportunity to observe situations that require ethical inquisitiveness and the ways in which others respond to those situations. It also offers an opportunity to respond to the environmental situations with an ethical determination. Typically, a sport environment will provide multiple occasions for ethical applications.

One of the most difficult responses to many conflicts is to do what one knows is the correct course of action. Upon reflection, individuals will typically know when a situation arises that challenges their moral principles. This is recognizing that a moral conflict exists that tempts individuals to disregard their moral principles. However, principled individuals will pause to consider how a response to a situation will reflect their values. Based upon this, a determination is then made on how to act. Lumpkin, Stoll & Beller (1994) refer to this as "to know, to value, and to act" (p.5). To know will require exposure to sound moral development, to value will require an understanding of personal beliefs, and to act will require the strength of conviction to respond in a way that may be subjected to criticism or ridicule (**moral courage**).

DEFINITION

MORAL COURAGE
requires that individuals stand up for those things in which they believe, as well as for those individuals who cannot stand up for themselves because they are in a vulnerable position i.e., children, mentally challenged, elderly, individuals who are dependent upon another, and risk retaliation including athletes, coaches, and others in the hierarchy of sport.

Moral Values

There are a number of moral values about which individuals need to determine their importance within their personal life (i.e., self, family) and social life (i.e., peer, athletic, school, work). The values of an organization and of the people who manage it will guide the development of its policy and related rules and regulations, and dictate how stakeholders are treated and expected to treat others. Examples of values include, but are not limited to, such attributes as honesty, responsibility, justice, fairness, impartiality, well-being, and integrity. Let's look at each of these individually.

Honesty is synonymous with truthful and sincere. Almost everyone would be likely to say that they value honesty. But when is the last time that you told a "little white lie," told a friend that you liked his/her new hair cut when you did not, told your parents that you were going to a friend's house when you did not, or you told a professor or a coach that you were ill or injured when you were not in order to excuse yourself from a commitment?

Do we value honesty only when we expect others to be honest with us, and not when we are expected to be fully honest with them? When does it matter? You must reflect on the value of honesty to you, and take responsibility for your actions. **Responsibility** is the next value we will study.

When we think of people being responsible (previously defined and also referred to as accountability), we expect that they are reliable and they will be accountable for their actions. Responsible people will make good decisions, and will be able to provide sound justifications for the choice they have made. We trust that responsible people will act in the best interests of those involved in a decision, and we expect them to do this consistently in a fair and just way. Now we will examine justice and fairness.

In sport, we see justice served in a variety of ways. When we talk about equity, we mean a form of **justice** that seeks to provide equitable opportunities to all, known as **distributive justice**. This may include distribution of resources, such as facilities and equipment, or accessibility to good coaches and support staff.

Justice is also practiced when making decisions and applying the rules and regulations. This is a form of **procedural justice**, and often intersects with legal decisions regarding sport. If there is a rule that prohibits athletes from using a particular substance because it is considered a performance enhancer, procedural justice must ensure that rules and regulations are properly applied when an athlete is alleged to have violated these rules. A simpler case would be the consideration of a sanction of an athlete for violating a team curfew. The athlete would need to know the curfew, have not met the curfew, presented his/her reasons for not meeting the

? EXERCISE #4
What role does self-indulgence play in each of these scenarios?
1. Friends
2. Parents
3. Professor
4. Coach

? EXERCISE #5
Explore specific ways where distributive justice is important in sport.

curfew and sanctioned (or not) accordingly. This sanction represents an example of **retributive justice**, whereby an athlete in such a circumstance would be sanctioned in a way that matched the seriousness of the breach. A fourth type of justice is **compensatory**, which is a form of righting a wrong that has occurred in the past. Using the example above regarding distributive justice and equity, compensatory justice may be achieved by providing access to support staff, i.e., athletic therapists, sport information or event management, that had previously not been provided equitably across a program. How does fairness differ from justice?

Fairness in sport has many examples and reflects some of the values already discussed. Fair can be considered honesty or justice. What makes fair a common word in sport i.e., fair competition, may be that it includes more than one aspect of moral values. Children might think taking turns is fair in sport. Yet as sport becomes more competitive, and the concept of winning becomes more important to both the most skilled and the less skilled on a team, taking turns or equal playing time may not be the fair decision for anyone involved. Fair in sport may mean abiding by the rules of a game, or receiving a fair/just portion of resources, treating individuals in an honest way, or being unbiased in decisions made. Fair is the collective application of positive values.

Being **impartial** requires that individuals are sensitive to the expectations of others, and that their decisions will be neutral, unbiased, and objective. It is important that we approach decisions with an open mind, recognizing that we all have had experiences that will influence (bias) the way in which we look at situations. Impartiality allows us to see other perspectives and either reaffirm our original viewpoint or establish a new one that might provide a better response to something that occurs in a new context. This is important to consider in fact finding and analysis of a conflict.

Well-being is fundamental to social values and is the principle of life, liberty, and the pursuit of happiness, which demands a concern for the health of individuals. In sport this can apply to a number of situations such as violence, regulations around safety equipment, use of performance enhancers, and gambling. The term often used to capture the essence of well-being is **beneficence**, which includes preventing harm, removing harm, not doing harm, and doing good. It could be argued that these principles are touted as the essence of a sport experience, and must be embedded in everything we do within sport organizations.

Ethical **integrity** means that people can trust that you will abide by the ethical principles that they believe you possess, and that they expect you to use in the ways that you behave. Their confidence in you as an ethical individual who is a good moral role model will strengthen your credibility in the duties that you assume.

Application of Ethical Terms

A review of the terms in Exercise #6 will be helpful in understanding the ethics of a situation and in determining the best way with which to resolve a dilemma within the sport environment.

(?) EXERCISE #6   Application of ethical terms.

1. **Means-end principle:** Those actions are right that treat people as an end and not merely as a means to an end. Commonly reflected in the phrase "the end does not justify the means."

Discuss how the following represents the means-end principle: An athlete whose goal is to win the scoring championship refuses to pass to team-mates, but expects to be fed scoring opportunities by team-mates.

2. **Principle of forfeiture:** A person who threatens the well-being of another, or uses another as a means to an end, forfeits their rights. In application, the sanction must match the seriousness of the infraction.

Discuss how the following represents the principle of forfeiture: An athletic trainer recommends to an athlete that they take a steroid to increase their strength in preparation for the upcoming season.

3. **Principle of universalization:** Equal respect is due all others unless an ethical reason exists for not doing so. In application, either everyone should follow the rules of a game, or no one should follow the rules of a game.

Discuss how the following represents the principle of universalization: The home crowd is provided with noisemakers with their paid admission at a championship event after the visiting team has been notified that there will be no noisemakers or banners allowed at the event.

4. **Moral agency:** Individuals should have the ability to set goals, the resources to achieve them, and the freedom to make unforced choices.

Discuss how the following represents moral agency: Two players on a team want to miss practice to attend a school sponsored theatre trip.

5. **Principle of equality:** People should be treated equally; however, if this principle must be violated, it must also be done equally unless a reason exists to do otherwise.

Discuss how the following represents the principle of equality. Two players broke curfew and were disciplined accordingly. Two weeks later, one of the initial two and two additional players broke curfew.

6. **Paternalism:** Another person(s) determines what is good for someone. This involves directing them to do something or preventing them from doing something. Weak paternalism can be justified on the basis of someone's inability to make a sound decision (age, knowledge, mental capacity etc.) while strong paternalism is difficult to justify because decisions are being made for someone who is capable of making their own decision and accepting the consequences.

Discuss how the following represents weak and/or strong paternalism. Two players on a team want to miss practice to attend a school sponsored theatre trip.

7. **Moral absolutism:** Some actions are good or bad regardless of the outcome.

Discuss how the following represents moral absolutism. A coach decides to play the best athlete who is recovering from a mild concussion in the final competition for the Provincial championship despite the advice from the athletic therapist that there is a risk of another concussion.

8. **Principle of double effect:** It is morally permissible to perform an action that has both a good and a bad effect if the bad effect is both unavoidable and unintended to achieve the good effect, and a strong justification exists for doing so.

Discuss how the following represents double effect. An athlete with a severe ankle injury would normally be kept out of the competition for recovery, but is faced with the decision of either playing injured or not playing in their last competition of their university career.

Summary

Sport is promoted as a way to teach people how to behave—time management, organizational skills, social interaction, and others—that will serve them well as adults, employees, and contributing members to society. Yet, at the same time the moral side of sport is often criticized for being corrupt. Rules are used and misused for the win and not respected as a principle of the game. Athletes are exploited for the win or for economic purposes. A number of terms have been used in this chapter that will guide your self-reflection and your response to ethical cases that will follow on a variety of topics. Find some of these terms in the following word search.

Ethical Terms

```
M  G  I  V  J  W  Q  Q  X  V  J  Q  M  P  L  V  F  A  I  D
K  Q  J  Q  I  U  D  R  J  Q  C  M  A  A  N  Z  L  O  W  I
E  C  N  E  C  I  F  E  N  E  B  M  I  L  G  F  W  J  S  K
E  Y  I  H  Q  L  R  A  A  G  T  T  C  N  S  X  N  B  Q  R
C  S  X  S  I  U  W  D  M  U  R  B  O  Y  C  H  P  U  H  L
N  E  M  Z  C  R  A  G  D  A  L  Y  U  U  U  C  C  K  I  E
A  L  O  S  W  I  K  L  P  R  S  Z  R  F  C  V  W  G  X  P
N  F  H  V  I  J  H  M  I  P  T  I  A  N  L  R  Q  P  R  P
O  I  F  A  F  L  I  T  J  T  T  C  G  W  Y  I  L  M  I  Q
S  N  Y  Q  A  Y  A  R  E  Y  Y  A  E  O  H  O  C  H  A  Y
S  D  Y  X  Z  D  U  N  D  F  B  S  S  V  I  K  O  G  F  M
I  U  Q  X  G  O  O  X  R  F  W  D  G  T  T  N  R  R  Y  B
D  L  E  C  I  T  S  U  J  E  B  Z  A  Q  E  C  M  J  D  K
U  G  C  C  E  P  N  L  K  I  T  T  N  S  K  Z  N  I  B  E
R  E  P  C  L  Z  W  Y  C  N  I  A  T  Y  X  V  Q  W  S  A
O  N  X  I  J  J  Z  V  A  O  C  Y  P  C  X  Q  A  J  E  V
M  C  X  B  B  Q  G  R  N  I  R  I  N  T  E  G  R  I  T  Y
Z  E  H  N  E  J  R  X  T  S  X  T  X  L  K  H  G  V  H  Y
V  S  R  S  W  T  Q  B  L  M  D  P  W  E  H  O  Y  N  Y  Z
Q  Q  J  S  Y  P  G  C  A  V  B  H  T  B  N  S  C  H  J  V
```

beneficence	honesty
courage	impartial
dissonance	integrity
equality	justice
ethics	NCCP
exploitation	paternalism
fair	self indulgence

Complete the following exercise.

Ethics:

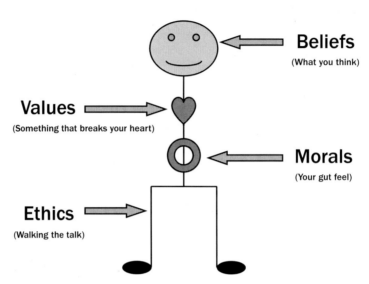

From *Making Ethical Decisions Course Facilitator Resources* by Coaching Association of Canada. Copyright by Coaching Association of Canada. Reprinted by permission.

(?) EXERCISE #7
Identify your six most important personal values in order of importance and explain why these are important to you.

Note: you must refer to this exercise throughout the course to guide your analysis on various topics.

Return to the statement, "fighting in hockey is good," which we will debate more when we discuss violence in sport. Apply the components of the Stick Man as a decision making tool. It may look something like this: In my head, fighting is good because it might draw more fans; in my heart, it is not good because someone is likely to get hurt or may not even play because they don't like fighting; in my gut I know it is wrong to engage in this behavior that is against the law anywhere outside of the game; so I have to stand up to the popular belief of my friends and speak out against fighting in hockey. In small groups, discuss how difficult this might be in the real world and how you feel about it. At this time, use the Ethics Stick Man to work your way through the analysis process.

This last step is one of the most difficult to take in every ethical decision. You will often have to speak out when no one else will, or when others are adamantly opposed to your beliefs. While you still can respect their position if they are able to provide a reasonable justification for it, you do not have to concede your position. This is known as <u>moral courage</u>.

Discuss in small groups a situation in which you observed someone who demonstrated moral courage. Be prepared to share one of your group stories with the rest of the class. You do not need to identify the people in your situation—make it anonymous.

> ❝ It is curious–curious that physical courage should be so common in the world, and moral courage so rare. ❞
>
> — *Mark Twain*

Notes

Lumpkin, Angela., Sharon Kay. Stoll, and Jennifer Beller. (1994, 2003). *Sport Ethics: Applications for Fair Play.* Missouri: Mosby.

Coaching Association of Canada. www.coach.ca

CHAPTER

Fair Play Principles and Codes of Conduct

❝ Richards banned: Former Harlequins' rugby director Dean Richards was banned from coaching for three years by a European Rugby Cup (ERC) disciplinary committee in Glasgow Monday. Richards resigned as Quins' boss last week after player Tom Williams used fake blood during a European Cup quarter-final against Leinster April 12 to create the appearance of a cut in his mouth in order to allow a substitute on to the field.**❞**

(*The Windsor Star*, August 2009)

⑦ EXERCISE #8

In preparation for this section, research mission statements and codes of conduct on the following websites and identify the ethical principles that they represent:

1. www.ofsaa.on.ca: Bylaws–Rules of Behaviour for Participants to OFSAA Championships, Code of Ethics for Coaches to OFSAA Championships, Code of Behaviour for Spectators

2. www.icce.ws/ethics (NCCP Code of Ethics)

3. The website of your primary sport and its code of ethics

   Provide a summary of what you found on the websites you researched.

Anyone involved in a sport likely will have signed a code of conduct or a similar document to confirm an understanding of the organizational expectations of members as well as an agreement to abide by those expectations which reflect the values of the organization. **Note:** the terms code of conduct, code of ethics, code of behavior will all be referred to as the same for the purposes of this section. At some point, you may be involved in interpreting, revising or even writing a code of ethics for an organization with which you assume affiliation. To accomplish such tasks it is important to understand what a code is, why it is necessary, what is included, and how it is implemented.

Code of Ethics

What Is a Code of Ethics?

- It is an expression of behavioral expectations of members (i.e., athletes, coaches, spectators).

- It represents the values of the organization.

- It represents the policy of the organization.

- It represents an acceptance of a mutual quest towards the goals of the organization.

- It communicates the importance of engaging in practices of fair play.

Why a Code of Ethics?

- Serves as an educational document.

- Provides guidance for decision making.

- Serves as a tool for evaluation of program and personnel.

Who Is Responsible to the Code of Ethics?

Everyone associated with a sport/sporting event is directly or indirectly responsible to the code of ethics, including:

- Coaches

- Athletes

- Support staff i.e., athletic therapists, managers

- Administrators

- Parents and other family members

- Officials

- Spectators

- Volunteers

- Media

- Sponsors

- Booster clubs

Content

As you will have noted in reviewing the codes to which you were referred in preparation for this class, there are some common elements. Most talk about respect. This includes respect for the athletes (team members, team mates, opponents) and their quest for setting goals and striving to achieve those goals, respect for the officials, and respect for the rules and the game itself (also referred to as honouring your sport). You will have noted the term **integrity** which includes characteristics such as honesty, consistency, responsibility and trustworthiness. Most sites also discuss **respectful relationships** which include those with parents and officials as well as colleagues (including rival coaches), and most importantly, athletes who cannot be exploited for personal pleasure (intimacy) or professional advancement (for the win). **Professional commitment** will be incorporated in some way to represent an obligation. For example,a coach has to be knowledgeable, current, prepared, and competent and athletes must train and compete according to team stipulations. **Honouring sport** is another component of many codes of conduct. This includes such practices as abiding by, not only the written rules of the game, but also the spirit of the rules to ensure fair play and competition. Honoring sport will be a significant ethical consideration for many of the topics discussed in this manual, such as contributing to a philosophy of drug free sport or resorting to the use of violence as a strategy in securing a win.

(?) EXERCISE #9

In your groups you will develop a code of ethics using the resources identified in this section. Predict where you will be ten years from now, and describe a sport setting where you will either be working or volunteering. Select one of these for your group. Based on the organization you have just selected, begin to develop your code of ethics by completing the Exercise #9 found in the Appendix.

One of the most commonly cited guidelines for codes that guide behavior is that of reciprocity, also known as "The Golden Rule". This principle, in layperson's language, is simply to do onto others as you would have them do onto you. In sport, we often feel aggrieved when someone interferes with our ability to achieve our goal, while we pay little attention when we interfere with an opponent's attempt to achieve his/her goal. We need to pay closer attention to behaving in ways in which we want or expect others to behave, and not behaving in ways in which we want or expect others to refrain from behaving. While an oversimplification, the implementation of this principle will contribute to making sport a positive experience for all.

The following list provides the top ten guidelines for fair play, as cited by elementary school students:

Guidelines for Good Sports-like Conduct (Entzion, 1991, p. 17)

1. Don't cheat.

2. Don't start crying every time you don't win.

3. Don't make excuses when you lose.

4. Try for first place.

5. Don't hurt anybody.

6. Take turns.

7. Don't brag.

8. Don't yell at teammates when they make mistakes.

9. Don't tell people that they are no good.

10. Don't kick anyone in the stomach.

? EXERCISE #11

Dealing with violations of a code of ethics–group exercise. Be prepared to share your discussions with the class. In preparation for this assignment, review the mission statement posted on line for your current educational institution and for the secondary school from which you graduated.

As an administrator of a school athletic program where the values of participation and competition are reflected in the educational mission of the institution, what are some of the ways that a code might be violated, related to the three following statements, and how would you make corrections?

? EXERCISE #10

Using what you have learned so far, what ethical commitment is involved with being an athlete?

What would you change in yourself as an athlete?

Repeat this question by replacing the word athlete with other roles such as coach, parent, teammate, or others.

CHAPTER ③

Youth Sport

In defining youth sport for this workbook, children, teenagers, and young adults are included in the settings of educational institutions, community programs, and club sport. Schools include elementary and secondary schools grades one through twelve, as well as colleges and universities. The latter have been included, even though sport programs at this level are typically viewed as exclusively for the highly skilled and elitist. However, the reality is that this will be the culminating competitive experience for almost all participants, after which most will compete more recreationally if at all. With this in mind and recognizing the value of winning, there only can be one ultimate winner, which suggests that there must be value in the sport experience for the many who do not win in order for them to continue their journey.

Recently, there has been a great deal of media attention given to the issue of obesity and lack of physical activity in our youth and the health related issues as a result of this combination. While elite sport seems to be thriving and opportunities plentiful, the reality is that many sports continue attempts to expand their memberships because girls and boys are not signing up for their programs or are dropping out. While reversing these trends requires a complex approach, one of the issues that we in the profession must consider is the friendliness of the environment we provide for young people in sport and physical activity. For example, an over-professionalism of youth sport may serve the talented few quite well, while alienating the majority who simply want to play to have fun, learn some skills, and be with their friends. As these attributes are fostered, the competitiveness will emerge for those with talent and aspirations, and provide the greatest good for the greatest number.

(?) EXERCISE #12   School sport philosophy.

Facts: A high school competes in an exhibition tournament to provide the team with extra experience. Throughout the tournament, three of the players were allowed play briefly in one of the round robin games, and two others did not play at all. All of these players have been committed to every practice and competition throughout the season. Four of the starting six played the entire tournament.

Issues: Identify the issues that raise ethical concerns based on the facts presented in this case.

Analysis: Discuss the following questions and complete the answer sheet located in Appendix A.

1. Why do high schools have varsity teams?

2. Why do high school teams compete in exhibition play?

3. Why do high school teams have more than just starters on a team?

4. Why might this situation be a problem?

5. Why might this situation be good for the team?

6. Why do high school students play on school teams?

7. Who is affected by the decisions made in this situation, and how are they affected?

8. What other ways might this situation have been handled?

9. Who might be upset about this situation?

10. Who should be involved in addressing the concerns that might arise from this situation?

Note: Review how these questions incorporate the strategies discussed in the introductory material that can be used for making ethical decisions (determine the facts, what are the issues, what are the pros and cons personally and organizationally, who are the stakeholders, what are the options, what action/decision should be taken).

A parallel issue to the physical well-being of young people in sport is the environmental setting in which we enroll our children that is deficient of ethical exemplars. Exposure to unethical situations through experience, observation, or media gives the impression that sport has evolved while the professed values have been eroded and the principles of fair play have vanished. Whether or not this is true does not matter. The fact remains that there are more boys and girls playing sport than in the past, there is a greater emphasis on performance at a high level, there are more parents and their children (including girls) dreaming of championships and playing on a professional team or a national team in their sport, and greater media scrutiny. While sport has never been free from deviance whatever the reasons, it appears that a segment of the sport culture may be more concerned about the role models to whom our youth are being exposed. One of the explanations for this might be that with more youth opportunities, there are more adults with or without adequate preparation, involved in the delivery of programs.

> Until the age of ten, children believe that success and doing well are based upon effort and social approval (Wolff, 2003).

Athlete Drop-out: Where Does Ethics Factor in?

There are a number of reasons for youth to drop out of sport and physical activity. These might be voluntary (other interests) or involuntary (cut from a team). Some of the most common reasons are that it is no longer fun, they are not skilled enough to continue, they decide to play another sport or take up another activity of interest (music), it is too structured/adult dominated, they have outgrown what is available, they are no longer interested, their friends are doing other things, or there is too much emphasis on winning. While many will argue that sport is about winning, it may be appropriate to reframe that statement. Everyone who enjoys competition also will enjoy winning and work to achieve the win. However, at what cost? By reframing the statement to say that sport is about setting goals and committing to the steps that are required to achieve those goals, the emphasis is removed from winning and placed on the process that is involved rather than the outcome. It is anticipated that there will be some weak paternalism in the development of goals, particularly when an individual's goals affect the goals of the collective or team, and in the knowledge and structure provided to assist people in achieving their goals. When working with youth who have the potential to develop into top level athletes, it is important for adults (parents, coaches) to use caution in the demands that are imposed on youth in order to avoid burnout.

Burnout can occur physically, psychologically, or socially. More than half of all youth will have dropped out of sport by the age of twelve years, many from burnout (Wolff, 2003). Physical burnout is often manifested by injuries, an outcome from overtraining or even overspecialization. Psychological burnout can occur from excessive demands or expectations placed on young people through pressure to achieve, failure to meet perceived expectations, or loss of confidence as they move to higher levels of competition. A sense of failure and diminished motivation can develop from an imbalance in the criticism compared to praise given, punishment drills, and verbal berating. Social burnout can occur when youth feel a loss of control over their lives and the time that they have to spend with family and friends and to be involved in non-sport functions that are fun and different. A feeling of missing out in these social events takes away from their ability to feel socially connected.

Proponents of youth sport believe that it is important for the development of character. However, this can be good or bad, dependent upon the ways in which sport is structured. Positive character development only can be achieved with well-planned leadership based on the mission of the organization. In professional or semi-professional sport, this is winning–in youth and educational sport winning is only part of a larger goal. It is the responsibility of leaders to teach respect for others, to develop physical and social skills, to instill an appreciation of a healthy active lifestyle, and to teach goal setting and a work ethic to achieve these. In the process, it also will allow those with special talents to achieve their ambitions, challenging all to reach their potential in multiple ways.

(?) EXERCISE #13
Children and sport.
Children play sport
to...
Children drop out of
sport because...

Sample Case Analysis

Case: As a department head in a secondary school, you must resolve a conflict between the junior and senior coaches of the basketball teams. There is a grade nine student who is an exceptional player. The senior coach wants the player to move up to the senior team, but the junior coach wants the player to stay with the junior team.

Analysis will include outlining the apparent facts and facts that are missing; identifying alternatives and the pros and cons of each; options available; and, a decision with justification. See Appendix B for a completed Sample Case Analysis form outlining this case.

Additional Cases

Using the principles outlined in the Case Analysis Form in the Appendix, analyze the following cases.

Case 1: A ten year old is consistently late for Saturday's 7 a.m. practice.

Case 2: A school decides to introduce a participation fee of $75 for those who want to play on interschool teams.

Case 3: A child in Grade 7 is doing poorly at school. There is no policy that requires a particular average for competing in co-curricular programs including sport. The coach is considering suspending the student from the team until the grades improve.

Case 4: An 11 year old playing baseball hits a single. The next batter then hit a fly ball that was bobbled and dropped by the short stop. The first base coach was screaming at the player to get back to first base (tag up) while parents were yelling at the player to run. The coach in the dugout ran out to the baseline and began yelling at the player. The player was caught between 1st and 2nd base and tagged out. When coming off the field, the father came out of the stands and was yelling at the coach and the player while the coach was still yelling at the player for costing the team an out.

Case 5: Ten year old hockey players join the team and are designated to the role of forward, defense, or goalie for the entire season. One of the goalies decided to quit the team because it was boring.

Case 6: A parent proposed a recommendation to the youth soccer league to eliminate heading the ball based on some research that speculates that youth players are unknowingly getting mild concussions as a result of heading that may have health implications in later years. The league is resisting the recommendation stating that heading is part of the game.

Case 7: A parent has been coaching in the league for several years. This year the coach requested and was given their child's team. Now parents are complaining that the coach's child is getting preferential treatment.

Case 8: A senior high school coach who believes that the team can make a run for the Provincial Championship has decided that the best way is to focus on the top six players with substitutes getting little practice time and no competition time. The coach believes that the top players need the extra time to be as strong as possible for playoffs.

Notes

Wolff, A. 2003. "The American Athlete: Age 10". *Sports Illustrated*. October, 59-66.

Introduction to Discrimination in Sport

Sport as a major social institution does not escape the cloud of discrimination that occurs elsewhere in society. It requires a recognition of discriminatory practices, actions to remedy injustices, and deconstruction of systems that traditionally have served to privilege a minority, typically white able bodied males in a small range of sports. A critical appraisal of the landscape of sport based on gender, sexuality, race, ethnicity, class, disability, age, and other possible delineations is essential to appreciate and understand the realities that underpin ethical debate. The following sections will address only a segment (gender, race and ethnicity, disability) of discriminatory practices in sport and the powers within sport that both endorse and resist ethical arguments for inclusivity.

There are a number of principles that apply to discrimination regardless of the context or the targets of the discriminatory practices. Again we see where social values of equity are reflected in the laws that have been designed at both the federal and provincial levels that place requirements on the actions of organizations and individuals. These laws have also guided the development of organizational regulations including sport, in an attempt to provide fair and equitable for all regardless of differences based on sex, race and ethnicity, disability, and others.

In spite of attempts to regulate actions, true change will not occur if it is not embedded in the values of the organization and each individual within that organization. As a result, meager endeavors often generate only token representation of minority groups. Justifications for failure to achieve diversity are complex but through an ethical examination, tokenism reflects an evasion of responsibility. This includes three primary arguments: first, that it is someone else's obligation to remedy the situation; or second, that it is either justified or not to be judged because everyone else does it thus making it acceptable or third, that it is no longer an issue as prior discriminatory practices have been resolved, blinding individuals to the ongoing discrimination and leaving it unchallenged. Each of these contributes to the potential for token representation of minority groups in sport based upon a characteristic(s) that is irrelevant to the criteria required for making a contribution to an organization. For example, being male does not mean that you are automatically a better administrator or being white does not mean that you are a better head coach. These concepts will be further analyzed within the discussion in the following segments on gender, race/ethnicity, and disability.

CHAPTER 4

Gender in Sport

> ** You can't build a reputation on what you are going to do. **
>
> — *Henry Ford (1863-1947)*

In preparation for this class:

1. Complete the Homework Assignments in the Appendix.

2. Google "Tennessee hostesses" and complete a summary form.

3. Explore the following websites: and record key points.

> www.caaws.ca
>
> www.tidesport.org
>
> www.acostacarpenter.org

Gender in sport has captured the headlines on multiple occasions over the past several years. Often the attention is associated with litigation built on the premise that organizational decisions have been unfair and discriminatory. Again we see the connection of social values with the laws enacted to protect the rights and privileges of our citizens. Interpretation for legal applications often can be connected to the ethical strength of arguments presented.

Gender and ethics in sport is a very general description of multiple issues that underlie the topic. Matters worthy of deliberation within an ethical framework are among others equal opportunity to participate, leadership opportunities such as administration, officiating, or coaching, career opportunities such as athletic therapy, sport journalism, sport information, or teaching and issues of organizational climate or environment such as harassment and sexual harassment, violence against women, inclusion, equal pay, or recognition. Again, any analysis must first

? EXERCISE #14
Reflection.

Part A: Provide three ways in which your experience with sport has been different than that of the opposite sex.

Part B: Select one experience with sport that you have identified in Part A and discuss any ethical breaches. Provide possible solutions.

examine the facts of an issue. From there, further analysis can guide a decision about whether or not there can be an ethical justification for the circumstances under debate. The research conducted by Lapchick et al. (www.tidesport.org, 2010) in their report card on gender in both educational and non-educational sport and that done over the years by Acosta and Carpenter (www.acostacarpenter.org, 1977-2010) that examines the statistics of women's status in American university sport both provide some critical facts. Homework Assignment #1 is provided in Appendix A to review Lapchick et al and Acosta and Carpenter research.

When you browse the Ladies Professional Golf Association (LPGA) website, you will find the following as the first paragraph:

> "LPGA-USGA Girls Golf provides an opportunity for girls, ages 7 to 17, to learn to play golf, build lasting friendships and experience competition in a fun, supportive environment, preparing them for a lifetime of enjoyment with the game. Girls are learning values inherent to the game of golf, such as practice, respect, perseverance, and honesty, preparing them to meet challenges of today's world with confidence."

After you have completed Homework Assignments #1 and #2, you will know some of the facts that make sport experiences and opportunities at all levels of involvement for females different from those experiences and opportunities for males, it is time to examine some of the grassroots issues through which you may have a possibility of influencing change.

⑦ EXERCISE #15

Use an ethical decision-making model to debate and analyze the following situations, including ethical principles to justify your ultimate position:

1. There are rule differences between the women's and men's game in hockey with respect to contact. The women play a "no checking" game where the men play a full contact/checking game. Why do you think that this exists? Do you consider this to be fair? Should the rules change for either the women or the men to make their games more similar?

2. Media coverage between female and male sport is dramatically different with approximately only 8 to 10% of the coverage reporting on women's sport, most of the writers are male sport journalists, and pictures of female athletes are more passive and sexualized than male pictures which tend to be aggressive action shots. How could you use ethical principles to advocate for a change in both the quantity and quality of the coverage of women's sport?

3. Female athletes are often sexualized through sport attire/women portrayed as sex objects not as elite athletes i.e., beach volleyball, figure skating, or cheerleading, while male athletes who participate in sports like figure skating are often labeled as "gay". Identify other situations in which **homophobia** creates

---

DEFINITION

HOMOPHOBIA An irrational fear and intolerance of same sex affection or sexual relationships that are a threat to the traditions of femininity and masculinity and challenge norms and traditions eg. Name calling, lack of respect for difference

an unfriendly environment for both male and female athletes. What ethical principles are violated in these situations?

4. Identify the facts that you believe have contributed to decisions allowing women to play in men's leagues, but men not playing in women's leagues. Debate this issue and determine an ethical justification for this to occur. Also work on an ethical solution that would provide an alternative to this type of integrated participation.

5. Captain College was in the process of hiring a coach for its women's volleyball team. In reflecting on its program, which includes eight sports for women and nine sports for men, there is only one female head coach (of 17) in the program and only one female assistant coach (of 38). In polling the team for their input, it was revealed that only two players had ever had a female coach. This prompted a review to see if this was common across programs. The majority of the female athletes had been coached by males much more often than females and in the hockey and soccer programs, not one athlete had ever had a female coach. The question now facing the athletic department is whether or not it should attempt to appoint a female as head coach of the volleyball team in an effort to create a more equitable staff based on sex of the coaches. Should female athletes receive most of their coaching from men or from women at all levels of competition? (Should male athletes receive half of their coaching from females?)

Facts to Help in Decision Making

- Historically, boys have had more and better opportunities in sport and physical activity than girls.

- Males have more opportunity for a career in sport and make more money when they are:

  - Athletes

  - Coaches

  - Administrators

- Females are more often relegated to supportive roles:

  - Hockey mom

  - Manager

  - Cheerleader

  - Hostesses

- Neither men's nor women's athletic programs in Canadian educational institutions are profit making enterprises. For example, university programs are typically funded by a student activity fee and facilities supplemented from general university funds (taxpayer dollars). There are more female students than male students to contribute to the activity fee. (**Note:** There is variation between campuses. For more specific information, research on an institution of interest would be necessary)

Summary

Decisions in sport and thus the way society views sport assigns greater status to males than it does to females. History can provide a partial explanation for this, but it cannot provide an ethical justification for it to continue. An examination of the gendered structure of sport too often places the focus on differences. But if you look at the people around you in this classroom setting, you are likely to have more in common with both the females and males in this course than you do with either the females or males outside of this course. Thus, if we shift our focus to the similarities that exist between females and males who have an interest, experience, and knowledge about sport, human movement and human behavior, we will be less likely to socially value sport based upon the sex of the individual but on the merit of the activity. This will assist in generating a more ethical perspective to guide decisions and actions.

CHAPTER (5)

Race and Ethnicity

Richard Lapchick, Director of The Institute for Diversity and Ethics in Sport (TIDES), has been the lead researcher in the publication of the *Racial and Gender Report Card* (www.tidesport.org). In the June 2010 edition, the report notes that:

> **"** The NBA continues to set the standard for the industry as the leader on issues related to race and gender hiring practices. As the 2010 Racial and Gender Report Card shows, the National Basketball Association had the best grade among the men's leagues for race and gender as it has for two decades. **"**

HOMEWORK ASSIGNMENT #3

In his report, Lapchick and colleagues report on the disparity between positions of leadership held based on race and ethnicity. While there are large disparities what is important is that positive change that has been occurring over an extended period of time. With the NBA taking the lead, it provides evidence that change can occur when the commitment to values of equity is a priority. Explore the information presented on www.tidesport.org and note points of importance that should guide ethical decision making by sport leaders.

Notes of significance from the highlights in the 2010 Report are:

The percentage of NBA head coaches of color _____.

_____ assistant coaches in the NBA were coaches of color.

_____ of the NBA's referees were white.

These findings are positive, but also reveal the need for continued vigilance to ensure that the change does not become a token representation but is embedded in the structure of the organization.

Media: In the quest for racial and ethnic diversity, attention is often focused on the competitive opportunities for participants. However, the lifelong benefits of sport experiences and the ethical implications for failing to address discrimination demands that career opportunities be central to the debate. Referring again to the work of Lapchick et al. (www.tidesport.org), an examination of the 2010-11 report of Associated Press Sports Editors shows significant disparity based on race and sex. Research the key findings of the report:

_____ of the sports editors were white.

_____ of the assistant sports editors were white.

_____ of the columnists were white.

_____ of the reporters were white.

_____ of the copy editors/designers were white.

Leadership: Likewise, a similar comparison of leadership roles suggests that people of color who seek leadership positions present a challenge for them. The leadership in the power structure of sport remains overwhelmingly white. Refer again to the website www.tidesport.org and research the following information on NCAA positions with respect to their racial diversity:

DEFINITION

NEGATIVE EXPLOITATION in sport occurs when winning and/or the means of winning often for other purposes such as money, become so important that the best interests of the individual (i.e. athlete, coach etc.) physically, emotionally, educationally, and psychologically or the organizational integrity are compromised.

Conference commissioners _____

Conference presidents _____

Athletics directors _____

Faculty athletics reps _____

Head football coaches _____

Faculty _____

Traditions are embedded in sport practices, many of which have been used to exploit people to maintain these traditions. Recruiting academically unprepared athletes for example, serves the commercial interests of a college institution for the purposes of program marketing and promotion for the generation of revenue. High athletic demands combined with low academic expectations exploit student athletes/athlete students for the benefit of the institution while potentially setting the student up for academic and career failure. Graduation rates of athletes (FBS) based on race is also worthy of review. The trend in football bowl teams is that the graduation rate for white athletes is much higher than it is for African-American players. A similar, but much smaller, gap exists when comparing female basketball players based on race. Exploitation based on race/ethnicity also occurs in other ways.

As you can see from the definition above, it implies that exploitation is not always negative. Athletes exploit a coach's expertise which has positive outcomes as the athlete moves towards achieving their potential. Adding to this scenario exploitation can be mutual when coaches recruit athletes to develop their talents further as a means to enhance their own career, i.e., higher salary, and a more challenging coaching position. Discussion about exploitation for non-moral reasons is further discussed in the section on commercialization of sport.

(?) EXERCISE #16 Making the invisible visible.
In a class on ethics in sport we attempt to make the invisible visible. We need to expose the facts, interpret the hidden or underlying messages or intent, and we need to reassign meaning based on respect for all. Consider the use of marketing strategies that exploit images for the promotion of an athletic program–the mascot debate (Case 1) and the application of rules to youth sport based on traditions (Case 2) using the following as a guide:

Case 1: Progressive University has had a caricature of a Native Canadian serve as their mascot for years. They have however, had few Native Canadian student attend their university and are unaware if there have ever been any Native Canadian athletes in their programs. The administration of the university has decided that it is time to change the mascot to demonstrate more respect for the population of Native Canadians represented through the use of this mascot. They are meeting with a great deal of resistance from alumni and from the public who claim tradition is important.

Case 2: A twelve year old girls' team has recently qualified for the Provincial championships. One of their girls is Muslim and has worn a head scarf throughout the season without incident. While the rules however, do not allow for the head scarf the local league preferred to have the girl play, be active and be with friends than to enforce a rule that prohibited her to play. The latter decision would have put her and her family unnecessarily in a difficult position based upon their religious beliefs, because there was no opposition to her playing with the head scarf. However the rules were enforced at the Provincial championships even though no one complained. The coach decided in consultation with the parents and the players that they would withdraw from the competition. The league then responded by making the team ineligible for playoffs the following year.

(?) EXERCISE #17 Support/opposition.
Apply the concept of how moral knowing, valuing and acting can work to examine racism in sport.

CHAPTER 6

Disability

As with other topics discussed in this workbook, issues concerning disability rights in sport are guided by legislation to reflect the values of society. Generally, these laws require consideration of a disability (i.e., physical, mental, learning) and accommodating individuals when providing services e.g., Ontarians with Disabilities Act (Ontario is the only province with disability legislation), or Americans with Disabilities Act. The Canadian approach has been more fragmented, incorporating legislation in policy dealing with human rights, employment equity or obligation to accommodation. A flaw in Canadian legislation, i.e., Canadian Charter of Rights and Freedoms applies only to those providing services to the public. So why is this a flaw? Would organizations not assume an ethical obligation to accommodate people with disabilities? Clearly as stated earlier, this is not the case and a reason for the need for laws.

Similar to the section on gender, sport serves as an institution that legitimizes discrimination. Women's and men's programs are often separate. Women compete on female teams and men compete on male teams. Likewise, sport is too often judged by physical prowess and performance for able bodied persons. Based on this perspective, accommodation of persons with disabilities becomes a low priority if any at all.

A relatively recent case in the game of golf received a great deal of public attention along with very polarized views. In the end, it required a determination by the courts to declare eligibility. In this case, professional golfer Casey Martin appealed to the PGA (Professional Golf Association) to use a golf cart in championship tournaments. The PGA rules did not allow this accommodation for any of the golfers, requiring them to walk the course in all rounds. Casey Martin had a debilitating leg impairment that made this impossible. The PGA and many of the golfers felt that riding in a golf cart changed the nature of the game and created unfair competition. One of their claims was that Martin's performance would be enhanced by removing the fatigue factor from walking that other golfers must overcome on their own. Martin proponents believed that the cart only allowed Martin to compete with other golfers in an equitable way because it helped him overcome a challenge that other golfers did not face.

The law is only as good as its enforcement, which is where the values of decision makers and the ethical commitment to those values become critical. Would you support Casey Martin in his bid to use a golf cart in tournament play?

Also, enforcement will not occur unless there is a complaint. Would you offer the opportunity to Casey Martin to use a golf cart in tournament play without first expecting him to file a complaint or would you proactively allow for such accommodations? Would your decision be different based upon the athlete's age, level of competition or sport?

There are many other cases with disabled sport and athletes that require critical ethical analysis. Assess the mission of the organization in the analysis of each case.

⑦ EXERCISE #18   Youth soccer.

Clarify the facts and identify the issues in the following example. Discuss the arguments that you predict would be presented to the league executive for both sides of the case. Even legal arguments will probably have an ethical grounding. Based upon the ethical principles that you have learned in this class (or elsewhere), place yourself in the position as a board member who must vote on a decision and state what you would do, providing an ethical justification.

A ten year old boy with cerebral palsy is mobile but requires a walker to support him while walking or running. He is fully integrated in his school classroom. When his friends talked about their registration for house league soccer, he asked his parents to register him as well. To play the game, he would have to use his walker. His parents agreed to register him, which they were able to do online. After the first meeting and game, two of the parents complained to the league that they did not think the children would be safe with him on the field using his walker and that he should be removed from the league. The league concurred, and informed the parents that he could be on the team but that he could not play in the games or participate in practice with his walker. The parents protested on behalf of their son with support from a number of other parents and many of the children who played games with him regularly in the school yard at recess and lunch time. The decision was reversed and the boy was allowed to play.

⑦ EXERCISE #19   School sport.

Clarify the facts and identify the issues in the following example. Provide ethical reasons to support these requests as well as ethical reasons to deny the requests (options). What would be your final decision? Provide justification, identifying which ethical principles are most important in the communication of your values.

OFSAA (Ontario Federation of School Athletic Associations) has eligibility rules that limit the length of time students can compete in school athletics. They may not be 19 years of age prior to January 1 of the start of school year, and they may not compete for more than five years from the start of their Grade 9 year. A student with a learning disability and born in the month of December who also played on the school's basketball team was progressing towards a high school diploma, but had spent an extra year in elementary school to catch up on the basics and then also spent an extra year to get the required Grade 9 credits and again to get the Grade 10 credits to be adequately prepared to handle the work in Grades 11 and 12. As a result, this student violated the age requirement in Grade 11 and the five year requirement in Grade 12. On both occasions, the student with parental support, team support and school support, appealed to the federation requesting that they waive the eligibility rules that would prevent participation on the school basketball team.

⑦ EXERCISE #20   Integrated competition.

For this case you will need to acquire some of the facts from www. paralympiceducation.ca and read about wheel chair basketball eligibility.

With the organization of paralympic sport and world class competition, disabled athletes have the opportunity to train and compete at elite levels while setting and striving towards goals. In some circumstances, there have been able bodied athletes compete with disabled athletes i.e., wheel chair basketball. Engage in a discussion about the ethics of this type of integration. Extend this debate to determine the ethics of disabled athletes competing with able bodied athletes in instances such as a blind distance runner who competes with a guide or an amputee who runs with a prosthetic. See posting below but consider other circumstances as well. Be prepared with an ethical response to either of these requests when they hypothetically register in a competition that you are hosting.

As technology advances and people with disabilities become more immersed in sport experiences, they too, will have dreams, goals, and challenges. Administrators and coaches will be faced with decisions based on new innovations. An example of this is the case of Oscar Pistorius who as a double amputee, dreamed of competing in the Olympics.

⑦ EXERCISE #21   Competitive aids.

Visit www.engadget.com to read more about this story (Prosthetic-limbed runner disqualified from Olympics by Joshua Topolsky). Complete an analysis of this case based upon your ethical knowledge and determine your position. If this were a request to compete in (a) university athletics or (b) high school athletics, would your decision be the same or be different?

CHAPTER ⑦

Commercialization

The role of money, television exposure, fame, material rewards, and sense of entitlement represent aspects of commercialized sport that often challenge our ethical decision making and lower the point at which we allow our values to be compromised. As stated by Lumpkin et al. (1994, 122),

> **"** Making money is not immoral, nor is commercialization immoral. When sport becomes <u>overly</u> commercialized though, athletes, coaches, and sport managers may be tempted to let a non-moral value like money, success, or fame influence moral decisions. **"**

What does overly mean?

Commercialized sport is embedded in North American society, and is extending its presence around the world. Professional and semi-professional teams operate as a business. Athletes, coaches, and numerous others who fulfill roles to make the business entity profitable are employees. Their interests are inconsequential, except as a commodity that contributes to business success.

Educational and youth sport technically do not fall within the business sport or professional model. They exist within an organizational structure that offers a different mission statement with concomitant program objectives (refer to previously researched educational mission statements). This is not to suggest that athletic programs do not want to win or do not want to make money. It is simply to point out that these objectives are not the primary role of the programs. Based on this understanding, sport organizations might approach decision making quite differently than a for profit organization. The remainder of this section will be dedicated primarily to the examination of ethical issues that emerge from college/ university sport. There is particular benefit in debating matters at this level of sport because it is elite competition and highly specialized. While it is not professional sport, there is a great deal invested in the delivery of these programs with

41

both financial and human resources. The result is a grey area between professionalism and non-professionalism. The adoption of a professional model of sport in a non-professional environment then becomes a source of ethical conflict and spawns behavior and decisions that are inconsistent with the organizational goals.

Begin by looking up the Ontario Federation of School Athletic Association (OFSAA) Bylaws Appendix IV, B32 at www.ofsaa.ca. This bylaw introduces the concept of **exploitation** within the educational mission of sport.

DEFINITION

EXPLOITATION

in sport includes
manipulation of rules
and/or people to
achieve a desired
outcome. It can be
either good or bad
but must always
be sensitive to the
balance of power
based on personal
or organizational
attributes. That is to
say, an athlete exploits
a coach's knowledge
to succeed is good.
A coach who exploits
athletes' talent and
continues to play
them when they are
seriously injured
because the win will
advance their coaching
career, is acting
irresponsibly.

Colleges/Universities (herein referred to as university)

Commercialization of university sport gradually established a dominant presence over the last 30 years or so on university campuses from coast to coast in the United States of America and more recently to a lesser degree, in Canada. As the stakes grow for both individuals and organizations, violations of ethical principles also increase. This is not to say that breaches in ethics did not occur in the 50s or even the 20s and 30s. It simply means that the volume of programs and the benefits, perceived or real, that result from winning provide the landscape for a greater number of abuses. For example, it is common to read about an institution being penalized for recruiting violations, academic deception, or general questionable behavior.

> " Tressel quits. Jim Tressel, who guided Ohio State to its first national title in 34 years, resigned Monday amid NCAA violations from a tattoo-parlor scandal that sullied the image of one of the country's top football programs. Luke Fickell will be the coach for the 2011 season. "
>
> (*The Windsor Star*, May 31, 2011)

Critics have questioned the graduation rate of some schools in some sports, and tutors have been found to complete the work of student athletes. So the following cases will allow students to explore the inside story of university athletics and the ethical issues that surface from time to time. In addition, the issues of performance enhancing practices and violence are sections that will be discussed separately, but under the umbrella of commercialization.

Note: You will now begin to see how the many topics covered in this workbook begin to overlap. For example, excessive resources going to one men's team can have a negative effect on women's teams and other men's teams. By the end of the course, you should be incorporating multiple critiques when making a decision on one particular issue. Decisions are never made in isolation of others.

HOMEWORK ASSIGNMENT #4

Prior to examining these cases, it is necessary to research some of the facts. This can be done by reviewing materials on the following websites and complete the worksheet at the end of this chapter to outline what you learned from each of these sites:

www.cis-sic.ca

www.ncaa.org (Particularly, review the posted Core Values and under Key Issues review the section on Commercialism.)

www.thedrakegroup.org (Review their mission, vision, and proposals.)

www.knightcommission.org (Review the Introduction, Principles, and Recommendations.)

Prior to examining specific cases, it is important to retrieve some of the relevant facts. The homework that you just completed should have accomplished some of that. In summary, the following are important points to understand. To the general public, the perception is that American college athletic programs are both financially self-supporting while in many cases, also supporting other athletic teams and even other non-athletic university programs. In Canada, the assumption may be that football and men's basketball support their programs with the revenue they produce. Either of these assumptions is disputable. It is highly unlikely that any athletic program in Canada supports itself financially when expenses of equipment, facilities, and their operational costs, competitive travel, coaching staff, support staff (marketing, administration, sport information, sport therapy, financial advisor, student support, and others) are factored into the budget. Similarly in the United States, budget shortfalls are the norm. Athletic programs on campuses across North America are subsidized by the university through tuition and fees and general university coffers yet even so, some institutions must bail out their athletic programs further due to debt incurred. In difficult economic times when teaching and research faculty are seeing wage freezes or cuts, heavier workloads and larger classes some coaches are rewarded with significant salary increases.

Universities, and particularly athletic directors, will argue the benefits to subsidies as an investment for the university. It allows them to offer a more diverse programming, particularly offering programs for women while responding to the law, that do not have potential to produce revenue. It is a way in which to generate interest from alumni and ultimately donations and to get students who will be the next generation of alumni involved on campus. The pride and affiliation with the university through athletic success provides a public profile that facilitates student recruitment and more tuition and grant dollars. Ultimately, a culture of membership and winning will attract public donors and corporate support.

From an ethical perspective, the question that must be answered is, "Where does the balance lie?" To produce revenue, there must be a winning team. But the winning team must also be football (a bowl game) or men's basketball (NCAA March madness). Canadian college sport has no parallel to these events. Nor do they have the population with only four regions across the country comprised of a total of 52 (2011) institutions. Thus, they do not have access to the substantial income generated by ticket sales, alumni donations, media, or corporate sponsorship. Attempts to adopt an American model of college sport requires extensive analysis, knowing that while there may be some good outcomes, there may also be some bad outcomes that must be managed. Often referred to as an athletics arms race, there is the assumption that spending money produces winners which requires more spending of money to continue to win. The reality is that there is only one winner (or a handful depending on the layered structure of sport–American vs. Canadian) raising the question of sustainability for those institutions that do not win.

Athletics historically have been valued as part of the educational experience on college campuses. Institutional support is not inherently a bad practice, nor is winning and subsidizations. However, now knowing that in almost all cases the athletic department's expenses exceed any production of revenue, what are the ethical issues that must be discussed and following a thorough analysis, what decisions need to be made by whom, and how can these decisions be implemented?

> **❝** Michigan State University men's basketball coach Tom Izzo makes more than $3 million a year. The Ohio State University that boasts the largest athletic department in the country spent more than it generated in 2009. **❞**

❓ EXERCISE #22   Athletics on campus.

Case 1: An assistant coach was recruiting for the upcoming season. One of the top players was not academically eligible to directly enter any university program so the assistant coach guaranteed the player a spot on the team following a year in a junior college for preparation. The player agreed, but over the year did not attend classes or succeed academically. However, when the time came to reconsider the player's university entrance, the assistant coach worked with the coach at the college whom he knew well, to have the grades adjusted so that the player would be declared eligible for the upcoming season.

Case 2: The team's alumni have become a major source of support for the growth of the program. They have worked with the coach and decided to create a separate organization at arm's length to the program itself. This would provide them with some autonomy on the decisions that they make and the activities they organize. They have generated a significant amount of money for the program to subsidize awards, equipment and to pay for an assistant coach. One of the athletes declined an offer by a recruiter from a rival institution since the alumni booster club was going to give them an award that paid all of their expenses. The rival recruiter understood that this was against league regulations and represented an under the table payment.

Case 3: A faculty member was concerned about the academic treatment of certain athletes in their sociology program. Two faculty members were allegedly providing passing grades to athletes who did not attend classes, did not complete assignments and on occasion, had been accused, but not found guilty of cheating on exams. A former team member admitted to receiving a grade of A in a course taught by one of the named faculty members without ever attending a class. In return, the faculty members were given tickets to competitions in prime seating and allowed to travel with the team to any post-season playoff competition unofficially as an academic advisor. The concerned faculty member raised the issue at a departmental meeting after which she experienced threats and sanctions. The stress resulted in a reduced performance and absences which then led to her dismissal.

Case 4: League rules require that teams be provided with practice time in the game facility when they arrive on site for a competition. The rules also prohibit observation or videotaping of an opponent's pre-competition practices for any reason including scouting purposes. Contrary to these rules, an assistant coach of the home team was found to be videotaping an opponent's practice and taking notes at the same time.

Case 5: A star player on the basketball team was in an altercation in the early morning hours with a neighbor following a party over the weekend which resulted in charges of assault. One of the arresting police officers called the player's coach as an alert to the charges. The coach went to the police station in the middle of the night to post bail for the player. The next day, the lawyer who had been provided by the coach, convinced the courts to postpone hearing of the case until the end of the season. While on bail, the coach continued to play the athlete.

Case 6: An assistant coach responsible for supervising study hall for the team's athletes regularly assisted the players with their course work. However, some players complained that the assistant coach was actually doing the work for the star players who then submitted it as their own. They also alleged that the assistant coach assumed the identity of the star athletes in online chats that were part of the grading structure for the course and completed their online assignments.

Case 7: Coach Ray has been coaching the basketball team for many years. He has had a great deal of success over the years. Because of his success and long standing at the school, he has a former player, Mr. Dean, who is now a physiotherapist and also an assistant coach. This assistant takes care of all of the injuries on the team as well as helping with the technical side of practices and competition. The team is again in the top three of the league standings and preparing for playoffs. There are three league games left before the quarter finals when one of his stars experienced a severe knee injury. Coach Ray told the player to walk it off for the rest of the game and to see the therapist after the game for treatment. Mr. Dean disagreed, and wanted to treat the athlete immediately during the game. Coach Ray said that he needed him to help on the bench and that the player may have to return to the game anyway because they needed the win. The player was left on his own for the rest of the game and did not get back on the court. Mr. Dean treated the player after the game, and during the next week but Coach Ray was insisting on the player participating fully in practices with the expectation of him playing in the next league game a week later. Mr. Dean opposed this, saying that the player needed to heal some, and that it would be better to have him for playoffs. This became a standoff.

Case 8: The athletic department enlists current students as volunteers to host athlete recruits when they visit the campus. The large majority of these volunteers are female, while the large majority of the recruits are male. The volunteers are trained about league rules. They are then given a budget to entertain the recruits, and told to provide them with whatever they need to have a good time. The volunteers are told which recruits are particularly important, and asked to provide them with a special experience. On occasion this has implied providing them with sexual favors and violating league rules by providing them with money or items.

Opponents

In preparation for competition the opponent is analyzed for strategic purposes, to help choreograph the win. They are not seen as personalities, but as inanimate objects that are attempting to achieve their own goals, while preventing us from achieving our goals. What is lost in this perspective is the fact that members of both teams are striving towards the same objectives–compete, perform the skills of the game, win, and enjoy the challenge. Yet, there are actions that suggest otherwise. Intentional rule violations (using an ineligible player) or other forms of cheating–running up the score, and improper language, for example "let's kick ass". Locker room pep talks often denigrate the opponent and fuel animosities.

(?) EXERCISE #23   Respect for opponent: Motivation strategies.
Identify a situation using competitive motivational techniques both prior to and during the contest that malign or belittle the opponent, and then discuss the ethics of this psychological strategy. Use some of the following ethical principles in your analysis.

Work a minimum of six of the following principles into your analysis:

Self-defeating test	Retributive justice
Beneficence	Compensatory justice
Responsibility	Universalization
Means-end	Forfeiture
Freedom	Equality
Moral courage	Respect
Moral development	

Sport is a mutual contest that requires the mutual respect of opponents since a competition does not exist without an opponent. Behaviors must reflect the purpose of the activity within the mission of the organization. It must be remembered that in most sporting contests, the athletes are central to the activity. While winning is always a desired end whether recreational, youth or varsity sport, it is only one of many. Winning is the outcome of preparation that tests the skills of one individual against the skills of another, either individually or collectively. The concept of winning at all costs becomes a source of questionable ethical actions that violates the spirit of sport when your opponent is the most important element that allows you to achieve your goals.

Officials

It is assumed that the officials will ensure fair competition. When the perception is that they are not fulfilling this obligation, we observe a variety of responses. Which one is the right one?

(?) EXERCISE #24   Officials.

A former high caliber athlete who retired from competition and decided to give back to the sport as an official spent six years in the process of deciding that he had had enough verbal and sometimes physical abuse from players, coaches, and fans/parents. He joined the approximately 30% of his cohort with this decision.

What are the issues in this situation?

What are the ethical principles being violated?

What are the outcomes?

What needs to be done in this situation?

? EXERCISE #25   Questioning calls.

Roger Federer is getting teased, and not just because he lost the U.S. Open last week. He is being mocked for his terrible eye. He challenged more calls in the U.S. Open than any other competitor, and yet he had one of the lowest success rates of any of the top players (Paul Kedrosky, Kauffman Foundation, September, 2009).

What do you think is going on here?

Identify unethical behavior and the ethical principles that support your analysis.

? EXERCISE #26   Parents.

A Little League baseball team of 10- to 12-year-olds was in a rebuilding year. Most of the parents sympathized with the children, recalling days when winning wasn't the only reason to participate. But then, it happened. A hit to the infield and a close play at first. "Out!" cried the umpire. "Kill the umpire!" cried a frustrated parent. "You're missing a great game!" shouted another fan. And the complaints grew in number and volume. Then, a voice came out of the stands from among the would-be umpire killers. "The umpire was right...it was a good call!" Silence followed. Slowly, parents turned around to check out the traitor who supported the umpire." (9)

Comment: The moral courage demonstrated in this scenario is uncommon, but needs to become more of the norm.

What are the issues involved in this case? Why do you think parents respond to their child's competition in this way?

What is wrong with this behavior?

What can be done to change the youth sport culture?

From *Strategies: A Journal for Physical and Sport Educators* by D.A. Ballinger. Copyright © 1992 by American Alliance for Health, Physical Educations, Recreation and Dance (AHPERD). Reprinted by permission.

? EXERCISE #27   Parents as coach.

A 16-year old baseball player volunteered to officiate in the younger divisions of his sport club. He was officiating a t-ball game, when he called a player out at home plate, a call that resulted in the team losing by one run. The coach ran onto the field and began screaming at the player (his daughter) for not sliding. The official intervened and ejected the coach. The coach proceeded to physically threaten the umpire until other parents entered the field to escort the coach away from the ball diamond. The coach was suspended for three games. The umpire quit officiating.

Why do people feel that they have the right to berate officials?

Apply your arguments to the above scenario including ethical principles to justify the position that you hold.

Some questions to guide discussion on fair and ethical expectations of officials:

- What are the values reflected in harassing an official? Use the cases cited above to identify some of these.

- Is it fair to expect a perfect job? Or should the expectation be that when players play a perfect game and coaches coach a perfect game, officials should officiate a perfect game?

- Can demands of officials be higher depending upon whether or not they are paid or on how much they are paid?

- Who has the right to evaluate officials? How and when should this be done?

- What are the effects of harassing officials?

- Is it appropriate for professional leagues to fine coaches and players for public criticism of officials?

Fans

The following are some scenarios intended to stimulate thought or the role of spectators at sport competitions. How far should fans be allowed to go in influencing the outcome of a game?

Case 1: In a girls' high school championship volleyball match, the opponent fans targeted one particular player for abuse, calling her by name as she executed every skill. They did this whether or not she was successful but more vociferously when she made an error. Eventually, the 14-year-old player's performance declined and she asked to be taken out of the game.

Case 2: A group of fans arrived at a competition with pots and pans to bang together and whistles to distribute to other supporting spectators. Other fans arrived with a variety of noise makers. The following year artificial noisemakers were banned from the competitive site for all sports.

Case 3: Visiting college basketball teams must go to center court during their time outs to hear the exchanges between the coaches and the players. In addition, the first few rows of spectator seating behind each team bench are lost in order to prevent spectators from interfering with game management on the benches.

Case 4: A family (including a four year old) of one of the players was in attendance at a varsity game. They had a long horn with them. During time outs, the horn was given to the four year old, and he was sent to the visiting team bench to blow the horn in their huddle. Most people laughed and thought it was cute. One individual approached the child and guided him back to his family saying that the visiting team was a guest in our facility and could not be treated this way.

(?) **EXERCISE #28   Disruptive behavior.**

At what point should someone intervene in fan behavior, why, and who should do it? What would be the ethical justifications for doing so? In answering these questions, review the table below and add any thoughts that you have. Then answer the preceding questions using ethical principles to justify your decision.

Is disruptive behavior ethically wrong?			
NO!		**YES!**	
Players need to be focused on their task. Fans have a right to get involved in the game. Fans may have paid to attend which gives them rights. All fans engage in this type of behavior – it is part of enjoying the game.		It is disrespectful of the game and the opponents. It interrupts enjoyment for others. Children model the behavior and use it in other contexts. More positive support helps the contest.	
Some ethical principles that may apply			
Fair play	Respect	Equality	Freedom
Self defeating test	Universality	Moral development	Benevolence
Forfeiture	Add others		
Provide your response to the question with your ethical justifications.			

CHAPTER

Performance Enhancing Substances and Practices

How Do Ethics Guide Our Actions?

> *"* Coaches take blame: Two coaches on the Brazilian athletics team are taking the blame for the doping of five athletes who were preparing for the world championships in Germany. Jayme Netto and Inaldo Sena said during a news conference Wednesday that the Brazilian athletes were given shots of the endurance-booster EPO without their knowledge. Netto and Sena said they were misled by a physiologist who said the amount of IPO being administered would not show up on doping tests. *"*
>
> (*The Windsor Star*, August 2009)

⑦ **EXERCISE #29   Who's who.**

In preparation for this lecture, attempt to find information about the relationship of the following to performance enhancing (PE) substances:

Who is: Ben Johnson?

Marion Jones?

Matt Baxter?

Jeff Adams?

Adrian Davis?

Barry Bonds?

Amanda Galle?

University of Waterloo football?

WADA?

CCES?

(Others may be added.)

One of the questions that needs to be answered is, "Why would athletes want to use performance enhancing techniques?" One of the simplest responses might be, why wouldn't they? So let's try to explore both of these questions from an ethical perspective. An additional question might be, "Why is approximately 80% of those violators male?" Keep this question in mind as you move through this section. It is also a question to discuss further when examining the section on gender, sport, and ethics. As noted in the introduction, topics in this workbook are inter-related. The use of PEs for example will include discussion on commercialization of sport, youth sport, and gender, over-emphasis on winning, fair play, and other topics and principles addressed throughout the workbook. Critical thought cannot be limited to an isolated debate.

Arguments Surrounding Performance Enhancing Techniques	
Pros	**Cons**
• There's a better chance of winning. • Everyone else is using. • It can equalize competition between countries with fewer resources for training. • It brings glory to the country/school with better performance. • It's more likely to achieve personal goals. • It requires less training time that can be spent studying. • It helps to avoid and recover from injury. • Some substances are not illegal. • It's just one part of a training program. • Reports of harm to health are exaggerated. • Good results may have economic benefits through career opportunities or sponsorship money. • Make it legal because too much money goes to enforcement. • Some testing is a violation of privacy.	• Health may be harmed & life shortened. • Not fair to those competitors who want to compete "clean." • It breaks the rules. • It does not represent a good role model for young aspiring athletes. • It is not an honest win. • If everyone uses enhancers, the advantage is lost (self-defeating test). • Spirit of sport is based upon fair play which is violated with use of performance enhancers. • It creates unequal competition. • Performances are artificial and records cannot be trusted. • It can have negative effect on others associated with the individual such as family and teammates. • There are high costs involved related to testing, i.e., research to stay ahead of rule-breakers, lab test costs, and expenses associated with out of competition testing. • There are Invasion of privacy issues.

The first question to be asked is whether or not there is a rule against using a performance enhancer. Some would argue that we use them all of the time in the advantages we seek with the creation of new and legitimate training techniques or advances in the efficiency of equipment. Others view performance enhancers as something that is ingested or injected to gain an advantage. Again, these may be legitimate. Examine the case of Mark McGwire, the former major league baseball player who played for the Oakland Athletics and the St. Louis Cardinals. McGwire received extensive media attention as he challenged existing records: (1) in 1987 as a rookie, he broke the home run record for rookies sending 49 balls out of the park; and (2) in 1998 he won an exciting race against Sammy Sosa for a new home run record by hitting 70 out of the park. There were suspicions at the time that his performance was receiving a boost from unnatural sources i.e., performance enhancers. These suspicions were countered by arguments that McGwire may be using substances that were designed to enhance his performance, but were natural products that were not on any banned substance list. Since that time, McGwire did in 2010, publicly admit to having used performance enhancing drugs throughout his career.

(?) EXERCISE #30   Before and after PEDs.

Surf the web and find pictures of Barry Bonds and Mark McGwire in the early and later stages of their careers and compare the differences in their physiques. Using this pictorial as a source of information, what have you learned about responsibility when discussing the topic of PEDs?

All records are a training and performance incentive as the top athletes strive to better those who preceded them. Following in McGwire's footsteps was Barry Bonds, who has a storied history but essentially has said that he unknowingly had taken steroids in the year (2001) that he broke McGwire's home run record.

From these examples one might ask: do records any longer have credibility? Is it cheating only if there is a rule against it? Is doping inherently unfair? Even if the rules allowed it, is doping ethical? Does the goal of fame and glory make it legitimate to take doping agents? Is it wrong to take performance enhancers only if you get caught? Why does it matter what anyone else is doing? Why do athletes feel a need to use performance enhancing substances, particularly those that are banned?

In tackling these questions, there are reasons an athlete might provide to justify his/her choices. They may know that there is a rule against it and are deterred by the risk of getting caught and suffering the consequences. This does however, not reflect a decision based upon their values unless it is purely in respect for regulations and the organizing body of their sport. There is also the lure of individual economic benefit through winnings associated with the sport, a potential professional career, or sponsorship money. Self-indulgence and placing a price on personal values will determine the extent that material benefits will influence personal values and choices. But there are also some organizational or structural influences on the decisions that athletes may make. The following points must be considered in ethical analysis and problem solving.

- Coaches who place unrealistic physical criteria on an athlete may contribute to an athlete's decision. For example, a football coach who evaluates an athlete in the spring training camp and tells that athlete that they must gain 30 pounds before the start of the season in August may encourage an athlete to consider steroids. Athletes who are training hard and eating well may otherwise have difficulty meeting this weight gain goal.

- Organizations who hire coaches who value the win over other organizational objectives, such as athletes' well being may indirectly pressure athletes to look for the short cuts to success.

- Providing incentives, such as money for winning gold medals, may be the push that results in an athlete's decision to get an edge through illegal performance enhancing techniques.

- Knowingly having members on a coaching staff who themselves have had a competitive experience that has been enhanced by supplements provides questionable role models.

- Failure to communicate a strong organizational position on the issue provides a questionable moral environment. Meeting the minimum league requirement of an educational seminar does little to express the organizational perspective. Strong messages must be conveyed that represent moral education reflective of the organizational philosophy.

- Violations and sanctions must be publicly communicated. Violators must be held accountable for the choices they have made while organizations must be accountable for the way in which they manage a violation, thus communicating their moral standpoint on the issue and contributing to the moral education of stakeholders and observers.

> **"** Jones' teammates want medals: Seven of Marion Jones' sprint-relay teammates ordered to return the medals they won at the Sydney Olympics, are raising money to legally challenge the International Olympic Committee's ruling. Jones last year handed back the five medals she won at the 2000 Sydney Games after confessing that she used steroids. LaTasha Colander-Clark, Andrea Anderson, Torri Edwards, Monique Hennagan, Chryste Gaines, Jearl Miles-Clark and Passion Richardson have formed a fund to pay for legal expenses to challenge the IOC's decision. **"**
>
> (*The Windsor Star*, April, 2008)

Everyone involved in sport has a viewpoint on the illegal use of performance enhancing techniques in sport. This viewpoint must be evaluated based upon personal values, organizational values, and the implications for the credibility of sport performances. In making choices, individuals must have the moral courage to make decisions based upon these values as well as standing up to those who are willing to break the rules for the purpose of self-serving interests.

Review the definition of self-defeating test previously studied and the sidebar definition of **Rights Test**.

(?) EXERCISE #31   Application of principles.

Apply these two definitions to an athlete's decision to use a performance enhancing substance on the banned list. Does your argument change if the substance or technique that the athlete is considering is not on a banned list? As an administrator faced with the appeal noted in the *Windsor Star* case

DEFINITION

RIGHTS TEST states that you have the choice to do what you want as long as it does not interfere with the rights of others.

reported above, use the NCCP model to analyze this request, and determine your decision.

Policy

Return to Chapter 1 and review what it said about the relationship between ethics and the law. You will find that the law is a reflection of social values. Likewise, organizational rules and regulations contained in policy and procedures are "laws" that reflect the values of the organization, for example, a sport organization.

The purpose of rules and regulations that emerge from organizational sport policy is to provide fair competition within the organizational philosophy. Anti-doping programs exist to preserve the integrity of sport and that which is intrinsically valued without influence from extrinsic and materialistic rewards. If everyone were to follow this principle, there would be no need for rules and regulations or the complexity of the policies that currently exist. Sport and the decision of whether or not to use banned performance enhancing substances and practices should be guided by fair play principles, honesty, personal well-being, excellence, good character, sound education and understanding, goal achievement and satisfaction with the journey, joy of competition, and overall, the spirit of sport for its own sake. In the process, the character development professed by sport leaders will be achieved: a sense of teamwork, dedication, respect for rules and people, commitment, courage, loyalty, and a sense of community.

The use of performance enhancing substances and techniques that are contrary to the written and unwritten laws of sport contravene the spirit of sport.

CHAPTER 9

Violence in Sport

> " Kugel 1ˢᵗ Spitfire banned from OHL. "
>
> (*The Windsor Star*, Saturday, October 27, 2007)
>
> " When He Is Bad... "
>
> (*Sports Illustrated*, October 29, 2007)
>
> " Let's kick ass. "
>
> (*Public statement at a high school competition. Speaker unknown, 2008*)

Violence and aggression in sport is always a hot topic. There has been discussion, research, and policy on the topic with difficulty in defining what is violence as well as ambiguity about tolerance levels and when enough is enough. The question of physical violence is itself difficult to assess. Its acceptability tends to change from sport to sport. But often psychological violence is overlooked – the intimidation factor. There are many definitions of violence and intimidation, but for the purposes of this workbook, we will use the following: Violence is the use of physical force used with the intent to injure another. **Intimidation** is a tactic used to frighten, threaten or inhibit another.

Another definition that has relevance in the discussions on violence is "gamestership", the practice of pushing the rules to the limit without getting caught.

There are a number of questions to keep in mind as this section is studied, both independently and in conjunction with other sections, as they will begin to connect. For example:

DEFINITION

VIOLENCE is the use of physical force with the intent to injure another.

DEFINITION

INTIMIDATION is a tactic used to frighten, threaten, or inhibit another.

What is violence in one sport compared with others?

What do the rules say about violence?

How does winning influence the use of violence?

How does gender influence the use of violence?

Who is responsible for determining the use of violence?

The "Everyone Else Does It" Argument

Those who defend violence in sport often will argue that it would be foolish not to include it in a game plan because it is part of the game. They argue that others will use it to gain an advantage and a coach would be irresponsible to eliminate it from the game plan. There are a number of ethical reasons that this justification loses strength, particularly in non-professional sport. The first question is: What is the purpose of sport in the context of the organizational mission? When you reflect on the material presented in the section on youth athletics, it is clear that most teams exist to develop skill, to offer competition in a social environment, and even to win, but not at all costs. A review of this purpose must at least plant the seed that violence has no role in sport. But, if this is not convincing, the next ethical principle that must be considered is honesty. Most sports have rules that prohibit violent acts and sanctions for breaking those rules, even fighting in hockey. These are the proscribed rules of sport, defining what cannot be done in the performance of the game. Players and coaches are expected to know and abide by these rules. Intentional violation of the rules changes the nature of the contest, and the game as agreed to at the onset of the competition no longer exists. The intentional violation of proscribed rules is, therefore, an act of dishonesty.

A third rationalization—to engage in violence because others do—is linked to winning. If you do not break the rules and exert violence to control the game, you are going to lose. From an ethical perspective, this should not matter and represents an overvaluing of winning and again an abandonment of the purpose of the sport contest in the first place. Further, if everyone uses violence in their strategies, the playing field has been equalized and there is no longer an advantage to violent actions (also apply self-defeating test). Since there can be only one winner, this approach of overvaluing winning defines everyone else as a loser, which again is contrary to the values that are promoted through sport.

To summarize the ethical debate around acting because someone else acts in that way even if it is unethical and contravenes the values of individuals or an organization, we must reflect (cognitive dissonance) on our own values. Someone must have the courage to change the course of this argument and expect through

DEFINITION

PRESCRIBED RULES are those rules that outline what you can do while participating in a competition.

PROSCRIBED RULES are those rules that outline what you cannot do while participating in a competition. Proscribed rules may get broken intentionally (an ethical violation) or unintentionally (a simple rule infraction and sanction).

example (moral role model) that others will follow. For those who honestly believe in their values and those of the organization, what others do does not matter. They will act according to their own values.

(?) EXERCISE #32   Intimidation and retaliation.

Apply what you have learned so far about the ethics of violence to the following case. Complete your analysis using the NCCP decision-making model.

Two rivals are meeting late in the season for their final league game against each other. The game means little because it already has been determined that these teams will meet in the first round of playoffs. However, in their previous two meetings, there were two opponents who continuously agitated each other, resulting in a couple of minor skirmishes and consequential penalties. This animosity continued in the current contest. Nearing the end of this game and encouraged by the coach, team mates, and media hype, one of these players who had fallen on the losing side of the early altercations entered the competition with clearly one objective–retaliating against the opponent who had been the cause of personal humiliation. This led to an act of aggression that injured the targeted opponent seriously enough to prevent the injured player from finishing this contest as well as participating in the first round of the playoffs.

The "Good" Foul/Penalty

What would you feel about the following situations?

- On a breakaway in hockey, the last player to help the goalie with defense trips the opponent.

- A player of the opposing team tries to take the ball from your player and the player takes a dive to encourage a penalty.

- In the last few minutes of a basketball game, a player intentionally fouls the opponent.

- Add two more situations from two other activities from sports with which you have had some experience, i.e., badminton, football, field hockey, lacrosse, and speed skating etc.

It is common for individuals to think that these situations are OK and players are in fact, coached to perform in this way. You are now being challenged to look at each of these differently and consider alternative approaches.

When we teach ethics in sport and physical activity, we are attempting to teach that there is value in the activity itself, which provides a motivation for acting according to the rules and expectations of the game or competition. Ethical individuals will want to abide by the regulations as well as the spirit of the rules because they value those rules, not because they are afraid of being penalized. While

While some may argue that fighting in hockey is part of the game, the rules in fact make it clear that fighting is not part of the game–there are specific rules against it and penalties associated with violation of those rules. **Prescribed rules** tell us what we can do when playing a game–in basketball you have 24 seconds to move the ball up the court and take a shot. Proscribed rules tell us what we cannot do without penalty. True, violations are inevitable, and thus proscribed rules have two categories. One is an inadvertent rule violation in which an individual in the nature of playing the game, unintentionally violates a rule of the game and accepts the penalty associated with that violation. The other is a deliberate rule violation where an individual intentionally violates a rule of the game to gain a specific advantage or prevent an opponent from gaining a competitive edge, i.e., scoring chance. This can be done with the understanding that they will be caught and penalized, but are willing to assume that penalty because it is in the best interests of the team. We see this occur near the end of a close basketball game when a player non-aggressively (or aggressively) fouls in the hope that they will regain ball possession in time to scramble for the win. However, it can also be done deceptively in the hope that they will not be caught and gain an advantage without having to take a penalty. This rule violation is the most disruptive to the ethical values of fair play.

When we talk about a good foul then, it truly is paradoxical. A foul is an interruption of the game. An intentional foul interrupts the game while changing the nature of the game. Individuals enter into competition expecting others to follow the rules of the game. Without that expectation, the potential for chaos emerges.

The good foul intentionally uses tactics that are proscribed by the rules of the game, which then changes the nature of the game. While many will say that proscribed rules are part of the game, the reality is that they are not intended to be part of the game. Over time, people have made them part of the game so that can be reversed and they can be removed from being part of the game. Like traditions, there are good traditions and bad traditions. Upon reflection, we need to decide what is in the best interests of the sport. What will keep children actively engaged in the sport? How will we provide a moral environment in which children/participants truly learn how to act in an ethical way?

Adaptation from "Why the Good Foul Is Not Good" from *Journal of Physical Education, Recreation, and Dance* by W. Fraleigh. Copyright © American Alliance for Health, Physical Education, Recreation and Dance (AAHPERD).

Violence and Contact Sport

While most sports have proscriptive rules against violence with designated sanctions to discourage the use of violence in sport, some sports are based upon violent actions against others or oneself, making it legitimate. These include such activities

(?) EXERCISE #33
Intentional violations.
Return to the situations cited at the beginning of this section, or to one of your own, and discuss how the explanation of proscribed rules applies to each. Include in your discussion the ethics of the action and the risk for harm to an individual or the game and its outcome as well as the potential benefit achieved. For example safety, fair play, and honesty may be factors. Identify others.

as boxing, ultimate fighting, mixed martial arts (MMA), and other relatively new extreme sports. Most people accept these sports as legitimate expressions of skill, power, strength, and competition without questioning the ethical implications. Others are critical based on the fact that they cause injury and even death. The number of deaths reported as a result of combat in the ring as best can be documented has been 21 in Canada and 751 in the USA, according to Svinth (2007). Wikipedia (2011) also provides some statistics on boxing deaths. Between the dates 1980-2010 (30 years), there have reportedly been 26 deaths, close to one per year with the first American woman reported to have died as a result of injuries from the ring in 2005. In contrast, MMA proponents argue that there has been only one death in their sport over a period of the last 12 years. Football is associated with the greatest raw number of catastrophic injuries for all sports, but the injury rate per 100,000 participants is higher in both gymnastics and ice hockey (Mueller & Cantu, 2011). In fact, soccer and gymnastics rank higher than boxing in the number of injuries documented, while football and scuba diving rank higher in sport fatalities. However, statistics fail to tell the whole story–these figures fail to communicate other debilitating outcomes, particularly neurological damage that interfere with the quality of life for those who have been subjected to regulated violence within a sport experience. Recent knowledge about the risk associated with repeated concussions in sport has captured the attention of health experts, sport organizations, and the public.

In addition to the injury and death issues that sacrifice the well-being and health of some individuals, other factors speak in opposition to the legitimization of combat sport. There are issues of exploitation associated with the economic production where the majority of those who suffer the physical abuse are least likely outside a few with exceptional talent, to financially benefit. Often, those who are recruited into the combat sports are those who are disadvantaged in other ways of life, while spectators lust in the entertainment of others being battered. And the hypermasculinity of the combat sports may contribute to the polarization of the sexes and the discrimination that continues to exist in other social settings.

On the other hand, sport is always a risk activity, some with higher risk than others. It is the excitement of this risk that attracts individuals to the sport. As a competition, it is a mutual quest for the challenge and the glory of the win, no different than any other sport. It is full of athleticism through which individuals test their strength and skill against another. The evolution of rules has enhanced the safety of participants with advances in equipment, organizational structure that includes careful medical monitoring before, during and after competitions, and emphasis is on the objective of scoring or superiority of moves as opposed to the harm inflicted on the opponent.

Therefore, this section is designed to stimulate thought and discussion about whether or not rules make violence and aggression legitimate. It is not intended as a lobby to ban such sports, but for students to understand the importance of critical thought about the ethical issues when making decisions to endorse these activities (i.e., what activities are legitimate, for whom, with or without modifications, in what settings?).

(?) EXERCISE #34   Support/opposition.
Using the ethical principles you have learned in this class, complete the exercise in the Appendix to determine two sides of the argument: support for boxing, opposition to boxing. Do your arguments change based on the sex of the participant, the age of the participant, or any other characteristics?

Mixed martial arts has gained recent popularity in spite of resistance from governments to provide sanctions for fights. However, recently the Ontario government has had a shift in their position, creating legislation that permits MMA in their province. Repeat the above exercise with MMA. Does your ethical position change based on the sport?

Hazing

DEFINITION

HAZING The Webster Dictionary definition of hazing is "to harass or annoy by playing abusive or shameful tricks upon; to humiliate by practical jokes; used especially by college students"

Hazing is included in the section on violence because it typically involves physical and psychological control, coercion, and ultimatums. Many of the activities involved in hazing are abusive, including physical violations that fit a legal definition of bullying, harassment and/or assault. Further, these demands are often characterized with sexual overtones that are degrading to females and gays, representing sexual harassment. Sexual harassment is illegal. Acts of homophobia may be classified as hate crimes.

There are many other definitions to be found in the literature on hazing. However, essentially in the world of sport, hazing is an initiation process for new members of the team to surrender themselves to the team and demonstrate their loyalty and submission of personal identity to the team, particularly the authority of the veterans. Historically, hazing has been a tradition in the hypermasculine sports such as hockey, football, and rugby. However, other sports, both male and female, have not escaped the induction of "rookies" through hazing practices.

In the United States, almost all states have specific laws that prohibit hazing practices. These have emerged primarily from the serious consequences, including deaths, of fraternity hazing. However, these laws also apply to the sport context. In Canada, there are no such laws. Hazing violates the law in other ways, such as underage drinking, unlawful confinement, indecent exposure, and assault. The following examples demonstrate the seriousness of some hazing practices and justify the need to ethically examine their legitimacy in the sport culture.

(?) EXERCISE #35   Hazing policy.

To begin this exercise, research policies on hazing in this institution, in Ontario University Athletics (OUA), and in one American university of your choice. What ethical principles apply to the following incidences of hazing? Some of the activities may include legal implications while others may not. Consider the role of all stakeholders in these situations and place yourself in the role of the sport administrator to determine if you should do anything based on your ethical analysis and if so, what those options would be.

Case 1: A university swim team (coed) planned a party after their first competition where it was determined that the rookies would be initiated. While it was said that the party was not mandatory, it was made clear that the party was a command performance for the first year swimmers. Each rookie was required to pay $10 to attend the party, and they (both females and males) were then told what they had to wear (diapers, bibs, a soother around their neck, carry a blanket or stuffed animal). The team had a pasta dinner where the rookies were required to prepare the meal for the veterans including the provision of alcohol. The $10 admission was used to purchase additional alcohol to be consumed by everyone throughout the evening. Much of the alcohol also was used for drinking contests between rookies and for punishments for losing planned games that the veterans organized for the rookies. Later in the evening of the initiation, a 17-year-old female rookie swimmer had to be taken to the hospital, where it was determined that she was suffering from alcohol poisoning and her stomach had to be pumped. The hospital then released the patient to the veterans who had delivered her to emergency, but who also had contributed to putting her at personal risk, promising to take care of her. The coach was not present, but had heard stories from previous rookie parties and had overheard some of this year's planning. The Athletic Director heard about the incident two weeks after it occurred through rumors.

Case 2: The football team had been practicing since the middle of July and played three of their league games by the time September 1st arrived. They convinced a university kinesiology student to volunteer as an athletic therapist to gain experience before returning to school to complete the final year of the degree program. The student had to leave the team prior to the end of the season, but the team wanted to hold a party for both an expression of appreciation and a farewell. During the party, there was lots of alcohol consumed with a number of tricks played on the student athletic therapist, who was the center of attention. The evening ended with the student athletic therapist stripped naked, tied to the goalpost on the team's football field and left for the remainder of the night. The first employee to arrive at the facility the next morning found the student athletic therapist and released the confining bonds.

Case 3: A familiar site for hazing is on a bus when returning home from an early season competition. One of the common male hazing practices is an activity known as the elephant walk. Others are the hot box, puck drop, and Dr. Broom. The hockey team veterans planned their early season initiation to include some of these activities and others on their way home from their first away game. The pranks began with the elephant walk in which the first year players were stripped naked, lined up to bend over and grasp the testicles of the player in front of them, walk to the front of the bus and back in that posture, while being subjected to paddling on the buttocks of veterans as they passed by their seats. The coaches were seated at the front of the bus. Additional hazing activities followed the elephant walk at the back of the bus.

Again, using the NCCP model, complete an ethical analysis with one of these three cases. Determine the role of athletic leaders.

There have been many hazing incidents in both American and Canadian sport. An examination of organizational values will determine whether or not you perceive hazing to have a role in your program. Respect for persons by itself will negate that possibility. With that decision, it is important to ensure a policy is in place, the policy and behavioural expectations associated with that policy are clear, communication of the policy including sanctions for violations is distributed, education and transparency are provided, and alternatives for inducting new team members are offered (team community work; special dinner provided by veterans to new recruits; ropes course; paint ball competition; participate as a team in another sport competition or charity function; or other opportunities that athletes design to legitimately bond in a positive way). If team members are involved in the development of positive activities to replace potentially harmful traditions, they will offer some exciting and memorable solutions.

Notes

Mueller, Frederick O. and R.C. Cantu, Robert C., "Catastrophic Sports Injury Research: Twenty-seventh Annual Report". Retrieved February, 2011, http://www.unc.edu.

Svinth, J. R. 2007. "Death under the Spotlight: The Manuel Velazquez Boxing Fatality Collection". Journal of Combative Sport. Retrieved February, 2011, http://www.ejmas.com.

CHAPTER (10)

Gambling and Sport

> *Soccer Scandal. A match-fixing ring with more than 200 suspected members fixed--or tried to fix--around 200 matches across Europe, in what UEFA called the biggest betting scandal in Europe. Bochum state prosecutor Andreas Bachmann said Friday initial estimates put the illegal gains at about US $14.85 million.*
>
> (*The Windsor Star Sports*, November 21, 2009)

The growth of gambling in general, and gambling in sport, specifically has some ethical implications for sport and its integrity. Pete Rose has been denied entry into baseball's sport hall of fame because of gambling activity and the perception that it may have a negative effect on the trust of fans, sponsors, coaches, teammates, opponents, and others in players to play to their potential and not adjust their performance to influence the outcome of the contest. It has been projected that illegal gambling permeates many sports (See "The Big Business of Illegal Gambling", www.cnbc.com, 2011 and www.ncaa.org). Football leads the way with $80-100 billion gambled in the National Football League, $6-10 billion on the Super Bowl alone. College football and basketball both rank high with illegal gambling activity. College football estimates are $60-70 billion wagered, while college basketball estimates are $50 billion. March Madness, the National Collegiate Athletic Association (NCAA) basketball National playoffs, have an estimated $6-12 billion of illegal wagering. The NCAA has recognized that sports wagering may be a problem within the student-athlete population, many who as college graduates continue with their gambling habits. Concerns with student athletes and their involvement with illegal gambling are that they are susceptible to demands of organized crime while jeopardizing their eligibility, their financial health, and the institution's reputation.

From an ethical perspective, if something is illegal it is, in all probability, unethical. This represents another example of the connection between social values and the law. Additional ethical issues are that gambling, particularly illegal gambling, can undermine the integrity of sport competition and can jeopardize the personal, financial and educational well-being of athletes and many others associated with the athlete and the program.

Animals for Entertainment: With and Without Gambling

Seldom when we think of harm in sport do we think of animals used for entertainment. Animals are used legally and illegally for the gambling entertainment of people. Many have attended and gambled legally on horse races or dog races. Integrity is lost when:

(?) EXERCISE #36
Animals for sport.
Based on social values, should it be legal for animals to be used for sport when the animal may be potentially put at some risk?

- The horses are whipped.

- The horses are drugged.

- The dogs are starved to make them run faster.

- The dogs are overfed to make them run slower.

Animals are used to entertain in other ways as well. There are often protests at the Calgary Stampede because of the perceived cruelty of animals in the chuck wagon races or the rodeo bronco where straps are tightened around the belly to make the animal kick. There are bull fights with the ultimate conquest being the death of the bull. And there are bull runs, cock fights, and fox hunts in the name of sport. One of the most notable legal cases that involved illegal gambling was the 2007 Michael Vick case. This Atlanta Falcons quarterback at the time admitted to conspiracy in dog fighting and helping to kill pit bulls at his property known as "Bad Newz Kennels". Following legal prosecution, Vick served a jail sentence for his activities and has since returned to play professional football.

> **❝ The greatness of a nation and its moral progress can be judged by the way its animals are treated. ❞**
>
> — *Ghandi*

CHAPTER 11

Organizational Ethics

Responsible Recruitment, Management, and Retention of Personnel: Being a Good Employer/Being a Good Employee

Organizational ethics involves more than ensuring that there is policy to guide decisions and measures taken to ensure individuals are in compliance with policies of the organization and the affiliated associations in which they have membership. It requires a mutual respect that creates an environment in which organizational effectiveness and innovation are maximized.

How do the following organizational decisions potentially affect a goal of achieving equity?

? EXERCISE #37 Administrative structure.
The existing structure of a college athletic program has a Director of Men's Sport (currently a white male) and a Director of Women's Sport (currently a white female). The incumbents work well together and share the workload, based upon the expertise of each. For example, one has an expertise in track and field so administers both the women's and men's programs, while the other has an expertise in ice hockey and administers that program for both the women and the men. When league meetings are posted with notices of motion, they sit down together to discuss the ways in which decisions will impact their respective programs and support each other with final decisions. When they cannot arrive at a consensus, both will compromise for the benefit of the program and its coaches and athletes. There is now a proposal for cost cutting purposes, to amalgamate the positions into one unit head with the title of Athletic Director who will have an Assistant Athletic Director Women and an Assistant Athletic Director Men. A further cost cutting proposal also is to amalgamate the Assistant

roles to one assistant for both women and men and title it Associate Athletic Director, responsible to the Athletic Director. Discuss which organizational structure would be the best choice from an ethical perspective, discussing the pros and cons of each, incorporating facts as you know them, and providing a full justification of your choice:

1. Maintain the structure with both a Director for the women's program and a Director for the men's program.

2. Restructure to have an Athletic Director with both an Assistant Director for the women's program and an Assistant Director for the men's program.

3. Restructure to have an Athletic Director with one Assistant Director responsible for both the women's and men's programs.

(?) EXERCISE #38   Administrative appointments.
An athletic department of a college has appointed a new Athletic Director to a five year term with the possibility of renewal for five additional years. There is a proposal to amend the term of office for the Athletic Director from the two five-year terms to a position of permanency allowing for an unlimited term of office. Discuss the effects of this principle of organizational structure based on an ethical set of guidelines.

Organizational ethics requires members of the organization to do more than comply with organizational policy. Members must also identify flaws in the policy, and ensure that policy continues to be developed over time to reflect the values of the organization as they change. Each member of an organization at any level is responsible for their own actions within that organization. Of particular relevance are the principles of respect, responsibility, and commitment.

Respect requires that individuals are respectful of others, themselves, and the organizational values and goals. Also, it includes a respect for the organizational assets such as finances, equipment, and other resources available to goal attainment.

Responsibility means meeting career obligations and expectations agreed upon when assuming a position. This may include such endeavors as professional development initiatives, working collaboratively with individuals both inside and outside the organization, abiding by organizational regulations, and remaining focused on organizational goals within its mission statement.

Outcomes will be measured, not only by their success within the boundaries of organizational goals—the what, but also in the means by which outcomes were achieved—the how. At this point, the ethical appraisal of an organization can be determined.

Creating an Ethical Organization

Leaders who model ethical behavior create an expectation of others to behave in a similar ethical manner. Ethical leadership will create an atmosphere of trust and respect, where others will be less likely to compromise the values of the organization. A sense of trust creates an open environment in which members feel safe to question or report behavior that violates the ethical principles of an organization. The outcome will be a reputable organization that will contribute to positive long term relationships and organizational success.

As part of the discussion in the preceding cases, creating diversity in your organization has many benefits. It offers diverse perspectives in decision making and program development. It provides a balanced and fair workplace which may be attractive to stakeholders, particularly those who see "themselves" within the organizational structure. And there may be financial benefits through the availability of special grant opportunities.

Policy is a starting point for defining the parameters of an ethical organization. However, the implementation of policy through such measures as hiring processes, programming, and creation of a positive workplace environment must also be present to achieve success.

Excuses will be made to defend unethical behavior even at the organizational level. Many of the arguments are the same as those used by athletes, coaches, spectators, and others within the sport industry.

⑦ EXERCISE #39 Excuses.
Provide a counter argument for each of the following possible excuses for unethical behavior in an organizational setting:

Most organizations at minimum, talk about equity in the workplace. They accept that discrimination in hiring and promotion, for example, are prohibited by law or organizational policy or in their absence, contravene the values of the organization. However, reflecting on the section of the workbook on discrimination, there is perceived legitimacy to decisions that fail to create diversity within an organization (review these). One will be the lack of qualified or experienced candidates from the minority group. A proactive approach to this challenge would be for an organization to contribute to the cultivation of a pool of qualified candidates recognizing that systemic rather than individual barriers limit progress to achieve diversity. Review the discrimination materials to understand why this would be a good approach for an organization. It may require creativity and an allocation of resources to achieve, but it will be an investment that is paid back to the organization in the long run.

Maintaining the Values of Your Organization

The first step of membership in an ethical organization is reflecting upon your own behavior. Ask yourself if you have ever:

- Cheated on an assignment.

- Taken something that was not yours.

- Referred to another in a derogatory way.

- Told a joke that demeaned another.

- Listened to a joke that demeaned another.

- Breached confidentiality.

- Knowingly breached a rule or regulation.

- Been less than honest

- Failed to admit an error

The first step is to recognize that none of us is perfect; we are only striving to be perfect! So you are beginning an ethical organization, you also have a responsibility to influence others, particularly if you observe behaviors that you classify as unethical. Begin by keeping the focus on you and proceed tactfully. You might begin by stating "I have a concern about this" or "I think we need to discuss whether or not this is right" which serve as ways to deal with the issue rather than the person. From this discussion, be prepared to offer alternatives to achieve the desired end. For example, "if we want to recruit the top field hockey player in the province, perhaps we could …" In other words, identify the goal and explore ways in which to achieve that goal using means that are both within the league regulations and ethical. If a solution is not found at this level, it is then important to enlist others to assist in the process. Such an approach is less likely to be confrontational and more likely to contribute to a healthy, productive and ethical organization.

> " Keep true, never be ashamed of doing right, decide on what you think is right, and stick to it. "
>
> — *George Eliot*

> ❝ It is not who is right, but what is right, that is of importance. ❞
>
> — *Thomas H. Huxley*

Additional Note: Research Ethics

Most organizations are involved in research of some sort to determine the effectiveness of their programs, the interests of their constituents or the viability of change. The research process involves striking a balance between the objectives of the investigative inquiry. It must recognize the rights and well-being of the research participants as well. While research ethics is a separate area of study, the following provides some basic precautions in an effort to protect and respect the research participants. When engaging in research that requires collection of information from people, the researcher should be attentive to the following:

- Provide sufficient information with an invitation to participate in the research so that a well informed decision can be made on whether or not to consent.

- When possible, provide anonymity (not knowing who participated in the research).

- Always provide confidentiality (knowing who participated only by the researcher while ensuring that the information provided cannot be linked to the research participant).

- Provide an opportunity for the research participants to access the results.

- Consider and protect the vulnerabilities of the research participant, i.e., based on age or mental capacity (Can they understand the research request and can they legally consent?)

- Always conclude with an expression of appreciation.

> ❝ It is far more difficult to do what is right
> than knowing what is right. ❞
>
> — *Author Unknown*

APPENDIX A

CASE ANALYSIS FORM

Case _____

REVIEW FACTS			
ISSUES	**ALTERNATIVES**	**PROS**	**CONS**
OPTIONS			
DECISION			
Ethical principles used to support your decision			

CASE ANALYSIS FORM

Case _____

REVIEW FACTS			
ISSUES	**ALTERNATIVES**	**PROS**	**CONS**
OPTIONS			
DECISION			
Ethical principles used to support your decision			

CASE ANALYSIS FORM

Case _____

REVIEW FACTS			
ISSUES	**ALTERNATIVES**	**PROS**	**CONS**

OPTIONS	
DECISION	
Ethical principles used to support your decision	

CASE ANALYSIS FORM

Case _____

REVIEW FACTS			
ISSUES	**ALTERNATIVES**	**PROS**	**CONS**

OPTIONS	
DECISION	
Ethical principles used to support your decision	

CASE ANALYSIS FORM

Case _____

REVIEW FACTS			
ISSUES	**ALTERNATIVES**	**PROS**	**CONS**
OPTIONS			
DECISION			
Ethical principles used to support your decision			

CASE ANALYSIS FORM

Case _____

REVIEW FACTS			
ISSUES	**ALTERNATIVES**	**PROS**	**CONS**
OPTIONS			
DECISION			
Ethical principles used to support your decision			

APPENDIX B

EXERCISE SAMPLE RESPONSES (please note that the responses offered to the exercises included in this workbook are intended to generate further discussion and additional potential responses and intended only as a guide.)

⑦ EXERCISE #1
Can ethics be taught?

NO	YES
Ethics classes are merely a fad	Ethics classes help students uncover their own values and reflect on what is important to them
Moral education is the result of applied training and practice, not abstract reflection	It provides an opportunity to cultivate an appreciation for moral behaviour
Contradictions between theoretical principles provides an excuse for avoiding moral decisions and actions	It provides a setting whereby students learn to recognize the difference between unethical and ethical decisions and actions
Moral justifications can be found to support actions to serve any desired behaviour	It highlights the importance of ethics
In reality, most people know good from bad and right from wrong – the challenge is responding to a situation accordingly	It encourages students to become moral leaders
	It provides an opportunity for moral debate and respect for the opinions of others
	Students learn how difficult it can be to be true to your values, particularly when faced with divergent opinions

(?) SAMPLE CASE ANALYSIS FORM

Players playing outside their age group.

CASE ANALYSIS FORM			
FACTS	Schools offer two teams, eligibility defined by age divisions. Both teams have set goals to be successful. One player has exceptional talent. Both coaches want this player on their team.		
ISSUES	**ALTERNATIVES**	**PROS**	**CONS**
Players playing outside their age group	Play within age group	Will benefit socially by playing with peers Will be a leader and role model for peers Will learn non-sport social skills Will have a chance to perfect skills May have to sit on bench as a senior Will get more playing experience Will have a chance to win awards Will help the team's chance of success	May not develop as much skill Juniors may resent a peer deserting them
Coaches unable to agree	Play outside age group	Reverse of above May have an exceptional team on occasion Allows a junior who would have been cut to play and a substitute to get more court experience A player this skilled will have lots of opportunity in the community to play at a more competitive level as a club player	Seniors may resent a junior taking a spot away from a senior Takes away from the development of a program with a junior program that feeds a senior program Seniors may not try out if they think they will be replaced by a junior
Department head has final authority	Let student decide		Student may feel pressure from coaches Student may not know what will be best for them

Student preference has not been considered	Let all players from both teams decide	Student will be happy so make more of a commitment Takes pressure off student	May only consider themselves
Effect on the success of each team	Allow the player to practice with the senior team and play the maximum number of games allowed by the league	Student gets extra coaching and play so good for student	Still displaces a senior Demands on the student become excessive Does not help the senior team win league play
Individual development vs. team development	Have the player join the senior team for exhibition play	Same as above	There are always exceptional cases that may be disadvantaged by a policy
Benefit to the student	Establish a policy	Takes the decision out of the hands of coaches and students or their parents Provides consistency across sports reflective of the program philosophy	
OPTIONS	1 – Keep the player within respective age divisions. 2 – Allow the player to play with the older age group. 3 – Allow the player to train and play with older age group with restrictions.		
DECISION	Option 1 – Keep player within the respective age group and compete with peers. This option provides the greatest good for the individual to learn how to win, to be a leader, to perfect skills, and be recognized. They will have time to be a senior and it will allow more seniors to have a positive experience with high school sport. For those seniors, it will not be likely that they will ever have a competitive experience like this again in this sport. Also, establish a policy that reflects the philosophy of the program within the educational mission of the school setting that avoids such conflicts in the future.		
Ethical principles used to support your decision	Equity, means-end principle, procedural justice, weak paternalism, universalization, beneficence,		

APPENDIX C

Exercises and Homework Assignments

Chapter 1 Introduction

(?) EXERCISE #1

Can ethics be taught?

YES	NO

What benefit(s) do you think you will gain from this class?

How will you achieve these benefits?

(?) **EXERCISE #2**

Fighting in hockey is good.

Provide arguments to explain why you **agree**.	Provide arguments to explain why you **disagree**.

(?) **EXERCISE #3**

Accountability in lacrosse.

What is accountability?

Explain the accountability of each of the stakeholders in the lacrosse situation:	
Penalized player	
Coach of the penalized player	
Coach of the injured player	
Officials	
Review Board	

⑦ EXERCISE #4
How does self-indulgence affect each of these scenarios?

What is self indulgence?	
How does self indulgence apply when you "tell a lie" or manipulate the truth to the following?	
Friends	
Parents	
Professor	
Coach	

(?) EXERCISE #5

Distributive justice in sport.

What is distributive justice?

Specific ways where distributive justice is important in sport: INSTRUCTIONS: You are to identify one (1) way where distributive justice must be implemented for sport to be fair and equitable. You are then to pass this to someone NOT in your group AND of the opposite sex to you who will **add one (1) more different** ways where distributive justice must be implemented for sport to be fair and equitable. Repeat this until there are six ways completed on the form and return it to its original author.

1.	
2.	
3.	
4.	
5.	
6.	

First Two Initials of Last Name: _____

⑦ EXERCISE #6

Application of ethical terms.

TERM	DEFINITION and APPLICATION	
1. Means-end principle	Define:	
	Application:	
2. Principle of forfeiture	Define:	
	Application:	
3. Universalization	Define:	
	Application:	
4. Moral agency	Define:	
	Application:	
5. Principle of equality	Define:	
	Application:	

6. Paternalism	Define:
	Application:
7. Moral absolutism	Define:
	Application:
8. Principle of double effect	Define:
	Application:

Group Name:_____ Student Identification Number: _____

First Two Initials of Last Name: _____

(?) EXERCISE #7

Your six most important personal values.

Value	Reasons
1.	
2.	
3.	
4.	
5.	
6.	

(?) REPEAT OF EXERCISE #2

Fighting in hockey is good. Does your view change at all?

Provide arguments to explain why you **agree**.	Provide arguments to explain why you **disagree**.

Chapter 2 Fair Play Principles and Codes of Conduct

⑦ EXERCISE #8
Codes of conduct.

Website	Key Content
www.ofsaa.on.ca	
www.icce.ws/ethics	
website of choice	

⑦ EXERCISE #9
Develop your code of ethics.

Sport setting _____ Your Role _____

          (e.g., gymnastics practice)   (e.g., parent)

Identify the values you perceive to be associated with that organization:

    We/I believe in the following values:

        _____ _____

        _____ _____

        _____ _____

        _____ _____

Determine ways to live these values as an organizational member:

    We/I will

        _____ _____

        _____ _____

        _____ _____

        _____ _____

(?) **EXERCISE #10**

Ethical commitment of an athlete.

What are the ethics to which an athlete commits?	
What ethical change would you make about you as an athlete?	
What are the ethics to which _____ (another sport role) commits?	

⑦ EXERCISE #11

Dealing with violations of a code of ethics.

1. A student's first commitment is to academic achievement.	
Violation:	Correction:

2. Coaches are expected to serve as positive role models for their athletes and for their school.	
Violation:	Correction:

3. Athletes are obligated to respect their opponent.	
Violation:	Correction:

Final question: From your experience, what would make a code of ethics more effective in sport?

1. _____

_____

_____

2. _____

_____

_____

3. _____

_____

Chapter 3 Youth Sport

(?) EXERCISE #12

School sport philosophy.

REVIEW FACTS			
ISSUES	**ALTERNATIVES**	**PROS**	**CONS**
OPTIONS			
DECISION			
Ethical principles used to support your decision			

ADDITIONAL CASES:

Case _____

REVIEW FACTS			
ISSUES	ALTERNATIVES	PROS	CONS

OPTIONS	

DECISION	

Ethical principles used to support your decision	

Case _____

REVIEW FACTS			
ISSUES	**ALTERNATIVES**	**PROS**	**CONS**

OPTIONS	

DECISION	

Ethical principles used to support your decision	

(?) **EXERCISE #13**

Children and sport.

Children play sport to...	Children drop out of sport because...	Solutions

Chapter 4 Gender in Sport

Class preparation summary form.

Website	Gender notations
"Tennessee hostesses"	
www.caaws.ca	
www.tidesport.org	
www.acostacarpenter.org	

(?) EXERCISE #14

Reflection.

PART A:

Provide three ways in which your experience with sport has been different than that of the opposite sex.

1. _____

2. _____

3. _____

PART B:

Select one experience with sport that you have identified in Part A and discuss any ethical breaches. Provide possible solutions.

Group Name:_____ Student Identification Number: _____

First Two Initials of Last Name: _____

⑦ EXERCISE #15
Ethical decision-making model

Case 1: Rule differences based on gender.

REVIEW FACTS			
ISSUES	**ALTERNATIVES**	**PROS**	**CONS**
OPTIONS			
DECISION			
Ethical principles used to support your decision			

Case 2: Media coverage.

REVIEW FACTS			
ISSUES	**ALTERNATIVES**	**PROS**	**CONS**
OPTIONS			
DECISION			
Ethical principles used to support your decision			

Case 3: Sexualization of female athletes.

REVIEW FACTS			
ISSUES	**ALTERNATIVES**	**PROS**	**CONS**
OPTIONS			
DECISION			
Ethical principles used to support your decision			

Case 4: Integrated sport.

REVIEW FACTS			
ISSUES	**ALTERNATIVES**	**PROS**	**CONS**
OPTIONS			
DECISION			
Ethical principles used to support your decision			

Case 5: Leadership

REVIEW FACTS			
ISSUES	**ALTERNATIVES**	**PROS**	**CONS**
OPTIONS			
DECISION			
Ethical principles used to support your decision			

HOMEWORK ASSIGNMENT #1

Examine the following chart. Fill in the blanks and add to the facts that need to be considered when making ethical determinations.

Lapchick et al. Website facts on gender	Acosta and Carpenter Website facts on collegiate sport in the USA
_____ of the sports editors were men.	_____ of women's teams are coached by a female head coach.
_____ of the assistant sports editors were men.	_____ of women's teams are coached by a male head coach.
_____ of the columnists were men.	_____ of men's teams are coached by a female head coach.
_____ of the reporters were men.	_____ of all teams (men's and women's) are coached by a female head coach.
_____ of the copy editors/designers were men.	When Title IX was enacted in 1972, _____ of the head coaches for women's teams and about _____ of the coaches of men's teams were females.
% (teams) of the women's teams graduated at least 50% of their basketball student-athletes. That compared to % (teams) of the men's teams.	_____ of athletics directors are females.
	_____ of NCAA schools have a full time sports information director yet only _____ are female.

Group Name:_____ Student Identification Number: _____

First Two Initials of Last Name: _____

HOMEWORK ASSIGNMENT #2

Research the administration of the LPGA (Commissioner; LPGA Player Directors; LPGA Independent Directors).

1. Are there ethical justifications for change? If so, what need to be the guiding strategies?

2. What else do girls (and therefore, boys) learn in golf and other sports?

3. What are the ethical implications of these messages?

Chapter 5 Race and Ethnicity

(?) EXERCISE #16

Making the invisible visible.

Case 1: Mascots

REVIEW FACTS			
ISSUES	**ALTERNATIVES**	**PROS**	**CONS**
OPTIONS			
DECISION			
Ethical principles used to support your decision			

Case 2: Religion

REVIEW FACTS			
ISSUES	**ALTERNATIVES**	**PROS**	**CONS**
OPTIONS			
DECISION			
Ethical principles used to support your decision			

⑦ EXERCISE #17

Support/opposition.

Summary. Apply the concept of how moral knowing, valuing and acting can work to racism in sport.

_____

_____

_____

_____

_____

_____

_____

_____

_____

_____

_____

_____

_____

_____

_____

_____

_____

_____

HOMEWORK ASSIGNMENT #3

In his report, Lapchick and colleagues report on the disparity between positions of leadership held based on race and ethnicity. While there are large disparities what is important is that positive change that has been occurring over an extended period of time. With the NBA taking the lead, it provides evidence that change can occur when the commitment to values of equity is a priority. Explore the information presented on www. tidesport.org and note points of importance that should guide ethical decision making by sport leaders.

Notes of significance from the highlights in the 2010 Report are:

The percentage of NBA head coaches of color _____.

_____ assistant coaches in the NBA were coaches of color.

_____ of the NBA's referees were white.

These findings are positive, but also reveal the need for continued vigilance to ensure that the change does not become a token representation but is embedded in the structure of the organization.

Media: In the quest for racial and ethnic diversity, attention is often focused on the competitive opportunities for participants. However, the lifelong benefits of sport experiences and the ethical implications for failing to address discrimination demands that career opportunities be central to the debate. Referring again to the work of Lapchick et al. (www.tidesport.org), an examination of the 2010-11 report of Associated Press Sports Editors shows significant disparity based on race and sex. Research the key findings of the report:

_____ of the sports editors were white.

_____ of the assistant sports editors were white.

_____ of the columnists were white.

_____ of the reporters were white.

_____ of the copy editors/designers were white.

Leadership: Likewise, a similar comparison of leadership roles suggests that people of color who seek leadership positions present a challenge for them. The leadership in the power structure of sport remains overwhelmingly white. Refer again to the website www.tidesport.org and research the following information on NCAA positions with respect to their racial diversity:

Conference commissioners _____

Conference presidents _____

Athletics directors _____

Faculty athletics reps _____

Head football coaches _____

Faculty _____

Chapter 6 Disability

(?) **EXERCISE #18**

Youth soccer.

REVIEW FACTS			
ISSUES	**ALTERNATIVES**	**PROS**	**CONS**
OPTIONS			
DECISION			
Ethical principles used to support your decision			

⑦ EXERCISE #19
School sport.

REVIEW FACTS			
ISSUES	**ALTERNATIVES**	**PROS**	**CONS**
OPTIONS			
DECISION			
Ethical principles used to support your decision			

Group Name:_____ Student Identification Number: _____

First Two Initials of Last Name: _____

(?) **EXERCISE #20**
Integrated competition.

REVIEW FACTS			
ISSUES	**ALTERNATIVES**	**PROS**	**CONS**
OPTIONS			
DECISION			
Ethical principles used to support your decision			

(?) EXERCISE #21

Competitive aids.

REVIEW FACTS			
ISSUES	**ALTERNATIVES**	**PROS**	**CONS**
OPTIONS			
DECISION			
Ethical principles used to support your decision			

Chapter 7 Commercialization

⑦ EXERCISE #22

Athletics on campus.

Case 1: Recruiting

REVIEW FACTS			
ISSUES	**ALTERNATIVES**	**PROS**	**CONS**
OPTIONS			
DECISION			
Ethical principles used to support your decision			

Case 2: Alumni

REVIEW FACTS			
ISSUES	**ALTERNATIVES**	**PROS**	**CONS**
OPTIONS			
DECISION			
Ethical principles used to support your decision			

Case 3: Academic Achievement

REVIEW FACTS			
ISSUES	**ALTERNATIVES**	**PROS**	**CONS**
OPTIONS			
DECISION			
Ethical principles used to support your decision			

Case 4: Scouting

REVIEW FACTS			
ISSUES	**ALTERNATIVES**	**PROS**	**CONS**
OPTIONS			
DECISION			
Ethical principles used to support your decision			

Case 5: Breaking the Law

REVIEW FACTS			
ISSUES	**ALTERNATIVES**	**PROS**	**CONS**
OPTIONS			
DECISION			
Ethical principles used to support your decision			

Case 6: Academic Performance

REVIEW FACTS			
ISSUES	**ALTERNATIVES**	**PROS**	**CONS**
OPTIONS			
DECISION			
Ethical principles used to support your decision			

CASE 7: Playing Injured

REVIEW FACTS			
ISSUES	ALTERNATIVES	PROS	CONS
OPTIONS			
DECISION			
Ethical principles used to support your decision			

CASE 8: Special Treatment of Recruits

REVIEW FACTS			
ISSUES	**ALTERNATIVES**	**PROS**	**CONS**
OPTIONS			
DECISION			
Ethical principles used to support your decision			

Group Name:_____ Student Identification Number: _____

First Two Initials of Last Name: _____

⑦ EXERCISE #23
Respect for opponent: Motivation strategies.

OUTLINE CASE			
REVIEW FACTS			
ISSUES	**ALTERNATIVES**	**PROS**	**CONS**
OPTIONS			
DECISION			
Ethical principles used to support your decision			

⑦ EXERCISE #24

Officials.

OUTLINE CASE			
REVIEW FACTS			
ISSUES	ALTERNATIVES	PROS	CONS
OPTIONS			
DECISION			
Ethical principles used to support your decision			

Group Name:_____ Student Identification Number: _____

First Two Initials of Last Name: _____

(?) EXERCISE #25

Questioning calls.

REVIEW FACTS			
ISSUES	**ALTERNATIVES**	**PROS**	**CONS**
OPTIONS			
DECISION			
Ethical principles used to support your decision			

Group Name:_____ Student Identification Number: _____

First Two Initials of Last Name: _____

(?) **EXERCISE #26**

Parents.

REVIEW FACTS			
ISSUES	**ALTERNATIVES**	**PROS**	**CONS**
OPTIONS			
DECISION			
Ethical principles used to support your decision			

(?) **EXERCISE #27**

Parents as coach.

REVIEW FACTS			
ISSUES	**ALTERNATIVES**	**PROS**	**CONS**
OPTIONS			
DECISION			
Ethical principles used to support your decision			

(?) EXERCISE #28

Disruptive behavior.

REVIEW FACTS			
ISSUES	**ALTERNATIVES**	**PROS**	**CONS**
OPTIONS			
DECISION			
Ethical principles used to support your decision			

Group Name:_____ **Student Identification Number:** _____

First Two Initials of Last Name: _____

HOMEWORK ASSIGNMENT #4

Summarize important information extracted from each of the assigned websites related to commercialization of college sport.	
www.cis.ca	
www.ncaa.org	
www.thedrakegroup.org	
www.knightcommission.org	
You will note that three of the four websites are American – provide some rationale as to why you think it is important to study these websites in the examination of Canadian college sport.	

Chapter 8 Performance Enhancing Substances and Practices

(?) EXERCISE #29

Who's who.

WHO	WHAT
Ben Johnson	
Marion Jones	
Matt Baxter	
Jeff Adams	
Adrian Davis	
Barry Bonds	
Amanda Galle	
University of Waterloo football	
WADA	
CCES	

(?) **EXERCISE #30**

Before and after PEDs.

OBSERVATIONS BEFORE:	OBSERVATIONS AFTER:

Significance of observations and responsibility of stakeholders:

(?) **EXERCISE #31**

Application of principles.

Self-defeating test:

Rights test:

Non-banned practice:

Case: Retributive Justice

REVIEW FACTS			
ISSUES	**ALTERNATIVES**	**PROS**	**CONS**
OPTIONS			
DECISION			
Ethical principles used to support your decision			

Chapter 9 Violence in Sport

(?) EXERCISE #32

Intimidation and retaliation.

REVIEW FACTS			
ISSUES	**ALTERNATIVES**	**PROS**	**CONS**
OPTIONS			
DECISION			
Ethical principles used to support your decision			

? **EXERCISE #33**
Intentional violations.

Situations:	Hockey trip on breakaway; taking a dive; basketball foul; two of your own situations 1. 2.
Proscribed rules:	
Ethical violations:	
Solutions:	

(?) EXERCISE #34   Support/opposition.

Using the ethical principles you have learned in this class, complete the the following chart to determine two sides of the argument: support for boxing, opposition to boxing. Do your arguments change based on the sex of the participant, the age of the participant, or any other characteristics?

FACTS and ISSUES IN SUPPORT OF BOXING	FACTS and ISSUES OPPOSING BOXING
OPTIONS (with pros and cons):	
DECISION and IMPLEMENTATION WITH ETHICAL JUSTIFICATION:	

Mixed Martial Arts has gained recent popularity in spite of resistance from governments to provide sanctions for fights. However recently the Ontario government has had a shift in their position, creating legislation that permits MMA in their province. Repeat the above exercise with MMA. Does your ethical position change based on the sport?

FACTS and ISSUES IN SUPPORT OF MMA	FACTS and ISSUES OPPOSING MMA
OPTIONS (with pros and cons):	
DECISION and IMPLEMENTATION WITH ETHICAL JUSTIFICATION:	

(?) **EXERCISE #35**

Hazing policy.

Organization	Policy highlights
Home university	
Ontario University Athletics (OUA)	
American university _____	

CASE ANALYSIS: SWIMMING, FOOTBALL, OR HOCKEY.

Case _____

REVIEW FACTS			
ISSUES	**ALTERNATIVES**	**PROS**	**CONS**
OPTIONS			
DECISION			
Ethical principles used to support your decision			

Chapter 10 Gambling and Sport

(?) EXERCISE #36   Animals for sport.

Based on social values, should it be legal for animals to be used for sport when the animal may be potentially put at some risk?

Facts and Issues: Ethical arguments that **support** this position	**Facts and Issues:** Ethical arguments that **oppose** this position

Provide your final decision, citing your primary ethical principles for justifying your arguments.

Chapter 11 Organizational Ethics

⑦ EXERCISE #37
Administrative structure.

Structure	Ethical strengths	Ethical weaknesses
1. 2 equal administrators		
2. 1/2 administrators		
3. 1/1 administrators		
Preferred structure with justification:		

⑦ EXERCISE #38
Administrative appointments.

Option 1: 5-year renewable appointment	
Pros	**Cons**

Option 2: Permanency	
Pros	**Cons**

Decision with ethical justification:

Group Name:_____ **Student Identification Number:** _____

First Two Initials of Last Name: _____

⑦ EXERCISE #39
Excuses.

ARGUMENT	COUNTER ARGUMENT
Everyone else does it.	When you honestly believe in your values and those of the organization, what others do ceases to matter.
Because I can.	
No one will know.	
(the leader) does it.	
It's not quite unethical.	
Rules are made to be broken.	
It's not my responsibility.	

Appendix D

Website Resources

Canadian Centre for Ethics in Sport: www.cces.ca

The Institute for Diversity and Ethics in Sport: www.tides.org

Australian Institute for Sport: www.ausport.gov.au

Coaches Association of Canada: www.coach.ca

Canadian Association for the Advancement of Women in Sport & Physical Activity: www.caaws.ca

Ontario Federation of School Athletic Associations: www.ofsaa.on.ca

National Coaching Certification Program: www.icce.ws/ethics

National Collegiate Athletic Association (NCAA): www.ncaa.org

Canadian Interuniversity Sport: www.cis-sic.ca

The Drake Group: www.thedrakegroup.org

Knight Commission on Intercollegiate Athletics: www.knightcommission.org

CASE ANALYSIS FORM			
FACTS	Schools offer two teams, eligibility defined by age divisions. Both teams have set goals to be successful. One player has exceptional talent. Both coaches want this player on their team.		
ISSUES	**ALTERNATIVES**	**PROS**	**CONS**
Players playing outside their age group	Play within age group	Will benefit socially by playing with peers Will be a leader and role model for peers Will learn non-sport social skills Will have a chance to perfect skills May have to sit on bench as a senior Will get more playing experience Will have a chance to win awards Will help the team's chance of success	May not develop as much skill Juniors may resent a peer deserting them
Coaches unable to agree	Play outside age group	Reverse of above May have an exceptional team on occasion Allows a junior who would have been cut to play and a substitute to get more court experience A player this skilled will have lots of opportunity in the community to play at a more competitive level as a club player	Seniors may resent a junior taking a spot away from a senior Takes away from the development of a program with a junior program that feeds a senior program Seniors may not try out if they think they will be replaced by a junior
Department head has final authority	Let student decide		Student may feel pressure from coaches Student may not know what will be best for them

Student preference has not been considered	Let all players from both teams decide	Student will be happy so make more of a commitment Takes pressure off student	May only consider themselves
Effect on the success of each team	Allow the player to practice with the senior team and play the maximum number of games allowed by the league	Student gets extra coaching and play so good for student	Still displaces a senior Demands on the student become excessive Does not help the senior team win league play
Individual development vs. team development	Have the player join the senior team for exhibition play	Same as above	There are always exceptional cases that may be disadvantaged by a policy
Benefit to the student	Establish a policy	Takes the decision out of the hands of coaches and students or their parents Provides consistency across sports reflective of the program philosophy	
OPTIONS	1 – Keep the player within respective age divisions. 2 – Allow the player to play with the older age group. 3 – Allow the player to train and play with older age group with restrictions.		
DECISION	Option 1 – Keep player within the respective age group and compete with peers. This option provides the greatest good for the individual to learn how to win, to be a leader, to perfect skills, and be recognized. They will have time to be a senior and it will allow more seniors to have a positive experience with high school sport. For those seniors, it will not be likely that they will ever have a competitive experience like this again in this sport. Also, establish a policy that reflects the philosophy of the program within the educational mission of the school setting that avoids such conflicts in the future.		
Ethical principles used to support your decision			